3 *ON,*
2 *OFF*

Rethink the 7-Day Week to Work Less, Boost Productivity, Increase Creativity, and Escape the Hustle

Linda Morgi

3 On, 2 Off: Rethink the 7-Day Week to Work Less, Boost Productivity, Increase Creativity, and Escape the Hustle

By Linda Morgenthaler

Cover artwork by: Kristin N. Spencer

ISBN 10: 3-9525736-1-2
ISBN 13: 978-3-9525736-1-7

On the web: 3on2off.com

Contact the author: linda@3on2off.com

To the liars and the bullies
Who will look
No, I didn't write about you
In this book
It's so nice to live my truth
I'm running free
If you'd only been honest
You wouldn't have to worry
About me

For Jeanette. Who always told me I wasn't the tiniest bit funny. I hope one reader laughs out loud to prove you wrong. You are the steadiest thing in my life. Thank you for being my rock. And even if you didn't read the pages, we can still use them as the world's most time-consuming dust magnet.

Table of Contents

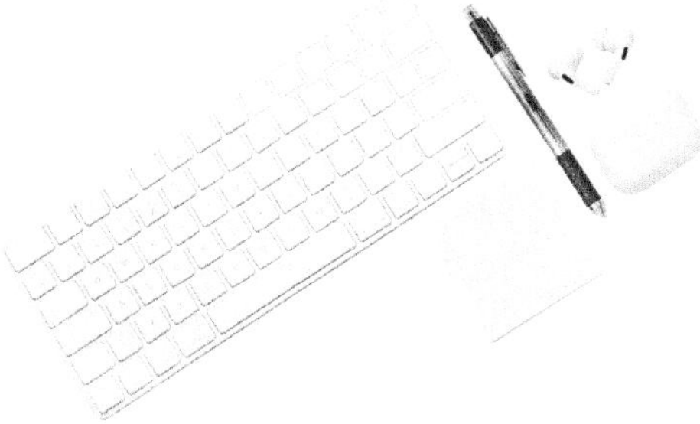

CHAPTER 1

It's Only Wednesday?

What if instead of having to count your work hours, you could make your work hours count instead?

Have you ever wondered if there was more to life than hustle and grind? Working both harder and smarter? Have you ever felt that dread in the pit of your being when the week already feels like it's been so long and hard and you realize it's only Wednesday? Or the frustrated anxiety you get Friday halfway through the day when you realize you haven't gotten the week's work done? Me too, but I couldn't take it anymore, so I decided to find a better way.

After years of forcing myself to work in environments that made me feel like a hamster in a wheel, working for hours and not going anywhere, I was finally ready to admit to myself that I was burned out and exhausted, and as a result, my health was nowhere near where I wanted it to be.

So, I decided to be brave: I abandoned that spinning wheel. I wanted to know what my options were. The truth was staring me in the face, and I knew I needed to make some drastic changes. On that journey, everything I thought I knew about work and the work-life balance totally transformed.

And now, in this book, I'm going to teach you how to forge your own path, too, and realize what it means to make Wednesday your Friday. Are you in? Are you ready to transform your workweek and your life? Amazing! Let's do this.

How It Started

Hi, my name is Linda Morgi and I'm a reformed hustle-culture enthusiast. Nice to meet you. There are certain things you just know about yourself without anyone else having to tell you. For me, it used to be that I loved to work hard, nonstop, because it made me feel like I was proving my worth. These days, when I look back at my life, I can see the damage that my work-until-you-drop behavior caused (and I'm mentally face-palming myself right now).

I've always been an overachiever. When I was younger, I sought admission to a university that was notorious for its low success quota just because I knew it would push me past my limits. I didn't care about the values of the curriculum (and didn't even research what they might be).

Honestly, I had completely bought into hustle culture and wanted to "rise and grind" my way to success every day. As I pursued my Master of Arts in Marketing from this internationally renowned university in Switzerland, a huge part of earning the degree was based on me pushing myself to accomplish the intense (and often unreasonable) workload: I had to write multiple papers while also working on my thesis and studying constantly.

It felt like one of the main objectives of my professors was to make us buckle under the pressure, and if we didn't, well then, we must deserve the degree.

Instead of being discouraged by the immense load of assignments and classes, I convinced myself I was thriving. And after graduation, I was determined to continue going on full blast in order to quickly advance my career.

I started in the sales department of an international consumer goods company. It wasn't my dream job, but I was ready to climb and claw my way up the ladder until I got to where I wanted to go. And from what I could tell, the way to do that was to put in hours. The higher the position was, the more hours the person doing it seemed to work. So, I put my nose to the grindstone.

Determined not to let my entry-level position discourage me, I showed up to my new career with a backpack full of motivation. And each new Monday, my backpack came with me. There was a problem though. I started to notice that over the course of each week, my energy and concentration would dwindle as the days droned on. I was putting in hours, but there wasn't much real work to show for them. By Thursday, there was not much left in that backpack.

Through the years, the companies I worked for varied, but the intense (and often underrepresented) work-hour demands stayed the same. The only thing that seemed to change was when the midweek slump would hit me. If the 50+ hours per week spanned across multiple weeks or work bled into my weekends, my productivity would fall off sooner and sooner in the workweek. It wasn't uncommon that I was dragging my feet and dreading the office by Wednesday, unconvinced I could make it to the weekend, let alone get everything done that needed to be finished.

As the years of this pattern added up, I felt less able to convince myself that my motivation-filled backpack was helping. I researched countless productivity methods to find ways to recharge myself—to no avail. Most days, I left the metaphorical device at home, unsure I would ever feel like picking it back up again.

Around this time, I had started to notice that I was changing, both inside and outside. My work hustle had initially been motivated by my career ambitions. But that didn't feel like enough of a reason to keep up my hurried pace anymore. My decreased motivation and dwindling happiness caused an interior alarm to go off. What was I doing to myself? What was I letting my workplace do to me? The rat race I had willingly inserted myself into started to make less sense.

Before I had started working, I felt optimistic about my future. But that had waned. I started to worry that my aim was too far from where I was. And sometimes I thought the target I was aiming at might be the wrong one entirely. I went from working to live (and enjoying life), to living for my work. I wasn't the broke college student anymore, but I had little time or energy left to enjoy my new (relative) riches.

In an attempt to revive my happiness and redefine my purpose, I founded a group class fitness studio as a side gig in 2012. Each evening, after I finished my corporate job, I trained people in a small setting and helped them find fitness activities that were enjoyable and time-efficient, which meant they would be able to stick to them and get in 2 to 3 hours a week of exercise, even though they were super busy. I also taught them how to find healthy, sustainable and nutritional eating options like I had done for myself. But building my own company next to my full-time corporate job added even more hours to my workweek.

The weekends were now time off from one job that I used to get necessary things done for my other job. And vacation time wasn't spent at the beach, but used as much needed time to build up my own company, which was constantly growing.

I expanded to 3 locations within the first 2 years. In order to save money here and there, I learned to do 99% of the build-outs myself instead of hiring contracted labor.

I learned how to build walls, insulate them, install tile, put in windows, and even build furniture from scratch. During that time, my workweek hours fluctuated between 50 and 90, with my workdays either bleeding into the weekends or fully engulfing them.

Because the work in my own business was of a different nature, I did feel less of a slump by midweek because the mix of activities would provide a small boost of energy again. But I noticed that no matter what I did, at the beginning of the week, my productivity was drastically different compared to the end of the week.

Fast forward through a couple years of juggling 2 different jobs, and the drain became too much to bear. I quit the corporate life in 2014, and went full-time with my own company, which had grown to include 18 employees. Over the course of the next 8 years, my working hours were typically still high, but I thought that was because I was an entrepreneur.

Every Thursday and Friday (and sometimes Saturday), I would drag my over-caffeinated self through the last things on my to-do list, only to collapse into the weekend, hoping I had enough time to recover so that on Monday my productivity levels would go up again. It was also common that I had to log into my computer or go and clean the facility on Sunday afternoon so that everything would be ready for each new Monday.

I kept thinking about a quote I had seen from Elon Musk where he said that no one had ever changed the world by working a 40-hour workweek. But I didn't know if that was the right way to look at my work life anymore. I had learned firsthand that hustle culture could only fuel so much energy and productivity.

How It Was Going in 2020

When the pandemic caused shutdowns in 2020, this led to major shifts in both my values and priorities. I found myself waist deep in a business I had started to turn my life around, which had now become another hamster wheel in disguise. The pandemic shutdowns threw a wrench into that wheel just long enough for me to stop and reflect.

At that point, my romantic relationship had been long-distance, spanning across 2 countries, for 3 years. Work had been a constant grind and a big pull away from my partner, which left me reeling from that absence emotionally.

If I had allowed myself the time to go see a doctor, I'm pretty sure I would have been diagnosed with the beginning stages of depression from all the burnout. I felt drained by the pandemic as a whole, and I couldn't juggle tasks anymore: at least not without risking my sanity and mental health. So, I decided to close and sell my brick-and-mortar business and move solely to an online model, founding 2 new companies. Not wanting to repeat my past mistakes, I was desperate to find a new way to work—productively and sustainably!

In this new adventure, I quickly realized that I could set my own schedule to mimic my spouse's shift hours so that we could enjoy more free time together. She worked a 5-day rotating model, where 3 shifts of a total of 24 hours of work were crammed into just under 2 days. That was then followed by 3 days off—with the first of those days spent recovering from the last night's shift. Then the format would repeat.

I adopted this same rhythm. This meant my schedule had me working 3 days on, followed by 2 days off, working another 3 days, and then having 2 days off again. Not having the traditional Monday through Friday workdays meant I needed to make some adjustments to the way I had done business before, but I immediately noticed that I felt a lot more focused whenever I was working.

Initially, I thought I would struggle to get all my work done since I had less total time available to work. This stemmed from the hustle mindset and my hamster wheel memories. But the opposite happened: With less time available, I was using it much better and getting more done. It was almost as if by limiting myself, I wasted less time. And best of all: I didn't have to discover a productivity hack or build a new habit. The external factors helped me achieve what all the hustle before hadn't!

The additional free time also felt amazing. It left

me feeling recharged and refreshed every 5 days. I kept asking myself, "Is this really it? Have I finally found the solution?"

For 15 years before this discovery, I had worked for 3 different corporate consumer companies, founded 3 different companies on my own, and worked a wide range of business models from back end to front end. I had been bound both to my desk and the people in the office, and had been required to do handiwork as well. I got to experiment will all kinds of work options to see which would allow me to work more productively and recharge. But this one worked the absolute best. So, I set out to investigate and test it.

The 3/2 workweek model I created based on my spouse's schedule shifted everything for me, and the results of my experimentation created the book you now hold in your hands. And yes, you can even use this method if you are a parent or guardian with children plugged into a traditional 5-day school week. (More on that later.) So, what does this look like for me today? Let me show you.

How It's Going Now—The Birth of the 3 on, 2 off (3/2) Workweek Model

The urge to write this book came to me as I was sitting at the local swimming pool, enjoying the sun on a Wednesday afternoon. It was peaceful there: so quiet. The weekend and evening crowds were blatantly absent. Half an hour before, I had finished my work. That meant I could enjoy free time with my partner at the pool. Yes, you read that right: I had finished my week's work in 3 days, meaning there were 2 free days ahead of me.

So, we went swimming—to take advantage of a midday, midweek time to skip the crowds who were still all stuck at work. But not simply because I shifted my work to remote. I implemented this work schedule in 2021. But the rest of the world was still in the fierce grip of the Corona virus pandemic.

Many employees found themselves forced into working remotely—something their bosses and employers had traditionally limited for years. The reason for limiting remote work was rooted in fear. The employers thought the employees wouldn't get any work done. But in the face of a global pandemic, they were forced to take that risk as non-essential workers were prohibited from going in to work in physical locations.

Contrary to popular belief, the working hours for those tuning in remotely actually went up, not down. The average worker clocked in 2 to 3 extra hours a day during the first lockdown[1]. That is over 12 additional hours a week!

Not only did the workdays get longer, but the work also bled into traditional off times and days like evenings and holidays[2]. At first glance, an in-home office might sound amazing. You don't have to battle against the ever-dreaded rush hour. You don't have to take sick days or a vacation day to go to a doctor's appointment. You can do laundry in the background while you get other work done. You can get the oven started with a delicious and healthy lunch during your conference call. But it's not as amazing as it sounds, and I'll tell you why.

The commuting time you save during the day and the availability for you to let the handyman in to fix your stove: those perks come at a cost. For every minute saved, another 2 or 3 seem to be added to the length of your workday. And it's not just you facing this problem, it's everyone.

Bosses suddenly feel fine sending out emails past 6:00 pm and expect prompt answers. The pre-breakfast calls start coming in before your morning routine is finished because your supervisor starts their day at 4:00 am. You go from working a 9 to 5 (honestly more like 8 to 6—more on that later) to always being just one ping away from a work request. This adds stress to home-office employees, and that stress starts to add up quickly. But don't panic. Let's head back to the swimming pool.

Now you know my secret, the 3/2 workweek schedule that allows me to visit the pool during the middle of the week during summer: when everyone else is at work. But what you don't know is that after testing this method, I realized I finally felt more satisfied with work, too. My productivity shot through the roof and stayed there. My stress levels shifted to an all-time low while my happiness soared to an all-time high.

It wasn't a change that happened because of a special productivity method. I didn't have to say goodbye to all my social relationships to make this happen. I didn't change anything about my task lists. And I didn't have to get up at 4:00 am to go through a magical morning routine to make this work. On the contrary.

Now, I take more days off. I add more weekend into my week. I work less. But I also get more done than ever before: and I'm happier doing it. But this solution isn't just for me. It will work for you, too. And in this book, I'm going to explain exactly why you should embrace the 3/2 workweek flow and what will happen once you do.

Let me ask you a question: Do you want your life back? Now is the time. Don't wait. Don't give into the false hype of hustle culture that this world wants you to buy into. Life has so much more to offer you, and I'm going to prove it. There's one last question I need to answer for you before I start showing you exactly how and why to make this happen in your life.

Who Is This Book For?

Before you dismiss this book because you think "I'm not an entrepreneur so this won't work for me" I want to tell you an important truth about the 3/2 workweek method. You do *not* need to be an entrepreneur, be self-employed, or be a remote worker to achieve the kind of happiness and productivity the 3/2 model offers. You read that right. In this book I will present alternatives to the outdated system build on 5 days on, 2 days off. Even if you are in a corporate job that still relies heavily on in-person work situations. Even if you are a parent. Even if you have few possibilities of working from home.

Now that you know a big part of my story, you know that I myself pivoted from an in-person position to completely remote. And I will show you how you can too, if that is your professional goal.

But even if you don't change anything about your current job, it is important for you to start thinking about yourself as an entrepreneur. When it comes to getting the most out of your work, this is the attitude you need to adopt. While it's true that someone can ask you to start work at 9:00 am, no one can force you to be productive. They might be able to shut down your access to Facebook and YouTube, but how you spend your time is still up to you.

This means that managing your productivity and increasing it is a job that lies solely with you. It is completely in your control and in your realm of influence. Let's look at 2 scenarios that illustrate what your choices really are when it comes to productivity.

The first scenario is that your workday is 10 hours

long (8:00 am to 6:00pm or 9:00 am to 5:00 pm with 2 hours added after the kids have gone to bed), and the time drags by because you don't feel connected to it, you can't focus, or you don't like doing it. You chip away, only to realize you made a mistake and now you have to go back and make corrections. You start something, but get distracted. And honestly, you'd rather take a coffee break with your co-worker, Andy (who is having network connectivity problems).

By the time you finish your afternoon meeting at 3:30 pm, you feel drained and decide there isn't much sense in starting another task so late in the day. So, you browse through your email and spend your time watching cat videos until your computer screen says it's 5:00 pm. At that point, you realize you really need to get task X done today, so you spend 75 rushed minutes on it so that you can leave by 6:15 pm. Just reading this scenario makes me tired. Thankfully, there is another one to consider.

In the second scenario, you work a day where you have 2 different meetings set up that last around 2 hours each. But instead of dreading the work you need to do in between, you're fired up to finish your tasks, the ones you've designated as the most important for that day, in between meetings. That way, by the time the clock says 4:00 pm, you have done all the important things you needed to accomplish in your workday. And after checking your email one last time—deleting anything you don't need—you're able to call it a day in time to go to your daughter's softball practice.

Which day would you rather have? For the purpose of simplicity, assume you get exactly the same amount of work done during both scenarios. Do you feel the same in both examples? If you're more interested in the second scenario, this book is for you. Keep reading. I'll help you get there.

If you prefer scenario one and you have a physical copy of this book, you can donate it or use it to prop up a wobbly table so at least it's of some use to someone. But don't bother reading it. I'm not interested in teaching you how to be stressed out or hate your job. And there are plenty of social media accounts with millions of followers out there that will gladly continue to feed your hustle narrative a lot better than I ever could.

My Goal for You Moving Forward

What I want to do for you in this book is leave you with all the options available to you that reduce your working hours and alleviate as much work-related stress as possible. Because, as you will see, if you don't find solutions that prevent workweeks over 40 hours, you will be forced to deal with massive health issues. That isn't what I want for you, and I'm sure you don't want that for yourself.

In this book, I'm going to show you how to increase your free time, how to use that free time so that you feel more refreshed, and how to keep things that way consistently. Ultimately, my goal for you is that you're happier. Happiness is what we, as humans, need. Happier people are more productive. Happy people are healthier in the long run. And more importantly: Happy people are much nicer human beings in general. If we are happy, we make better daughters/sons, moms/dads, co-workers, friends and traffic participants. As you will see throughout the rest of my story, it is my opinion that happier, more productive people, lead more fulfilling lives. And who doesn't want that?

How to Use This Book

In this book, I wanted to give you every single tool you could possibly need to make this amazing method work for your life.

At the end of each chapter, you'll find a section called "Key Takeaways" that will give you a list of condensed points that I went over in that chapter.

There are also QR codes that link to worksheets so that you can learn more on specific topics that interest you. You can either scan the QR code below to get your worksheets or go to www.3on2off.com/extras. You'll be asked to enter your email so that I can give you access to the members area where all the tools you'll need to take action based on the 3 on, 2 off method are conveniently located in one easy-to-find place.

The quotes I've written (or chosen) that head each chapter are small food-for-thought moments to tune your state of mind for what's to come. As you read each one, take a minute to reflect on what comes to mind before you move into the chapter.

You'll also notice a lot of stories in this project. I find that stories make concepts and points easier to remember, so I've included plenty. These tales either belong to me or my clients. You will notice as we go along, I'm pretty good at making mistakes. I've written some of the big ones here. The best thing about that is you don't have to make the same ones I did after I share mine!

You will also see headings within the chapter that read "Time to Reframe—_______" where I tackle wrong assumptions we (or our bosses) have about the workplace. The most important thing for you to know about these sections is that they are going to challenge what you've been taught in traditional schools and in some corporate work situations. Your brain might protest because breaking old patterns and beliefs is difficult. That's okay. All I ask of you is that you remain open-minded. As this book builds, you're going to notice a pattern that will it make it easier for your brain to understand these reframes. I promise.

You can either read this book from cover to cover

(which should take around 6 hours), or you can skip around using the chapter titles or Key Takeaways to read what is most applicable to your life right now. Here is a quick breakdown, but feel free to refer to the table of contents at any time.

Chapters 1 through 6 offer an introduction and analysis of the 40-hour, 5-day workweek, the way productivity has been studied in the past and how that is currently changing, experiments in a shorter 4-day workweek, increasingly popular remote- and hybrid-work models, and the effects of people working too much on both mental and physical health.

In chapter 7 you will see the 3/2 workweek method explained and get access to how you can create a model or variation of it in your everyday life.

The remaining chapters deal with implementation on both macro and micro levels and also use case studies to show what these practices can do to create a healthier, more satisfying, and more productive workplace.

It is my hope that, through this journey we're on together, you'll become part of rethinking our traditional workweek, work environment, and lead the needed changes. Thank you for giving me the opportunity to share this method with you. It changed my life, and I know it can change yours too.

Yours truly,

Linda Morgi

CHAPTER 2

The Problem with Our Productivity Measurement

Who is the winner in a race to the top of a mountain: The guy who started running earlier so he could take his time, or the guy who walked faster?

Working at a fast-food restaurant wasn't my favorite. But as a high school student with no driver's license, I didn't have much of a choice. And I definitely preferred it over listening to howling toddlers who hadn't wanted to go to sleep at my previous babysitting job (bonus tip: The dinosaur clip from Disney's "Fantasia" on repeat worked wonders).

At this food chain, everything had an exact way it needed to be done. I can still remember the movements and instructions. Shake the fries twice when removing from the fryer, tilt and drain the extra oil for 5 seconds, shake again, and salt with 4 shakes. If a customer comes through the drive-in, you have 90 seconds from the start of their order to taking their payment. At the regular counter, you have 120 seconds. And so on. Those time increments were how employees were measured.

If you were too slow at a station or job role, you got rotated to another one (or yelled at to go faster until you did). Since I was one of the few that had grown up with the local language, I usually got stuck with working the drive-in (because deciphering the orders through the awful, cheap microphones and headphones was difficult enough without a language barrier).

As a free-spirited, independent soul in progress, I found only one satisfactory way to deal with the micro-specifics that the restaurant job required: I had to find a way to beat the system. So, for each new order, I set out to beat the 90-second deadline. Not only would I take the payment for the order, I would also serve it. I wanted each transaction to be the fastest of the entire shift. Every single time.

Completing such specific goals gave me a rush of accomplishment. It made sense to me. And that's when I realized: In fast-food settings, the happiness of the customers seemed to be in direct relation to how fast they got their items. As long as they got everything they had ordered the exact way they had ordered it, faster was better.

The annoying thing was that if I did everything faster and was waiting for the next order, I would get scolded by my boss for loitering. But I had already completed all of the needed the tasks! That's when I started to realize that not everyone thinks about productivity in the same way.

Looking through the lens of fast-food efficiency is how I first saw the truth about productivity. In that world, it was all about how long it would take you to complete a given task. When I got my first job after university, well, that was a different story.

At my next job, no one really had a clue what you got done or how fast you completed it, but they knew exactly how long you were inside the office. The focus shifted from what you could accomplish to how many hours you spent at your desk. I was used to measuring what I could do in 90 seconds, but this was a whole new world. I had entered into something called hustle culture.

The thing about hustle culture is that everything centers on being seen and being present. It has little to do with how much you get done. (Because honestly, who really knows if you never miss a single deadline?) In the land of hustle, more time must mean more productivity. And standing around taking a break is a waste of resources, right? As it turns out, it's not that simple.

Time to Reframe—Productivity: Being Productive Is Not Just About Getting More Done

When you open up any dictionary, you'll usually see this kind of definition under the word productivity:

> *The resulting effects of effort that produces one or more outcomes, usually in a given industry, being measured by how fast the output can be accomplished, usually in specified units.*

In concern to work, the general understanding of productivity applies to how much work you can get done in the hours (or time) you work. A formulaic representation looks like this:

$$\text{PRODUCTIVITY} = \frac{\text{WORK OUTPUT}}{\text{WORKING HOURS}}$$

The Formula for Productivity

The most important thing to notice about this formula is how the work output is measured in direct relation to the hours put in. How much you can get done while working a certain number of hours has been an indicator of performance for decades. In most jobs, getting more done (faster) is automatically considered to be better. So, it seems logical to focus on this measurement when thinking about how to identify success.

Over the years, the demand inside jobs and on the workforce has gone up. Self-improvement guides on productivity have become widely popular. We have all been trying to get more done within the hours we have to work, and just to make sure that happened, work hours increased.

Because of the emphasis on increasing the amount of work we accomplish, a lot of more modern methods tried to point people to change from working on one thing at a time to multitasking, and when that didn't work, they advised going back to focusing on single-tasking. Ever-fluctuating approaches point to the fact that these attempts at higher productivity aren't doing everything employers want them to do.

In fact, the amount of varied advice we have on what exactly can create higher productivity is baffling. In one method, proposed in his book *Getting Things Done*, David Allen teaches that we ought to organize tasks into focus areas and have at least 3 different task lists so we can pull up the correct one according to our situation or location. To create contrast, in his books on minimalist methods, Leo Babauta suggests that simplicity is the answer. Yet another approach is found in *Eat the Frog*, where Brian Tracy advocates doing the most awful or dreaded task of the day first—before you can convince yourself to avoid it. In a similar way, in her book *The 5 Second Rule*, Mel Robbins encourages you to just get moving and start. But just getting started is not the only problem these guides try to solve.

We also see methods that take out or bring in relaxation: Janet R. Lee promotes limiting your breaks and any non-work downtime activity. She also suggests reducing your sleeping hours. Other methods like Francesco Cirillo's Pomodoro Technique prefer taking a planned 5-minute break every half hour before you get a longer one later. What all these strategies have in common is that none of them actually explain the change we need in order to shift our thinking about productivity.

Most of the books I just listed explore the same ideas over and over again. The only levers they want us to pull to increase our productivity seem to be differing task organization techniques and increased work hours. We work longer to try to have bigger outputs.

It's like taking a racing horse on yet another sprint, around and around the track, because it wasn't fast enough during its first few laps. Surely someone who understands how fatigue works or who cares an ounce about that horse wouldn't attempt something so cruel. So why do we do it to ourselves with working hours?

The truth is, few productivity gurus have talked about how to foster a better mental state for increased work flow and productivity. Cal Newport calls this "Deep Work," which is also the title of his book. His method centers around learning how to focus on one's work without distraction. Something most of us are not used to: Everything around us is trying to distract us. The first rule of marketing is to capture attention. And our phones, computers, and streaming apps have great ways of doing that, especially when our tired brains are overworked and under-rested.

Being able to produce focused, highly-effective work is a much-needed quality that will be required by the workforce of the future, especially because innovation and creativity must continue in order for progress to be made. And I'll tell you a secret: This will also produce more high-quality work in fewer work hours.

While the *how* has been the focus of few, the long-term effects of longer hours, more stress, and higher expectations seem to have been completely disregarded by all the productivity methods that depend on increased hours and constant task appraisal. Too few experts have looked at the sustainability of their productivity measurements as the hours stack up over weeks, months, and years.

Using the wonderful logic found in math, when we look at the productivity found in each additional hour worked, we need to average at least the same amount of output per hour when additional time is added to the workday. Otherwise, the productivity doesn't stay the same: It actually decreases. Unfortunately, the formula that is usually used to consider output doesn't consider anything but hours. Results are left out of the equation entirely.

PRODUCTIVITY = WORK HOURS

What We Think Productivity Is

Time to Reframe—Productivity and Health

In the long run, when the health of employees suffers, so does their productivity. Any model that is truly productive must take sustainability into consideration.

Let's think about that horse again. Let's say you flog it enough to win the cup today, only for it to fall dead of exhaustion tomorrow—never to race again. Is that really a long-term win? One of the most valuable questions of all concerning productivity is: How can the measured output be sustained over months, years, or decades?

Instead of using hours as the only number that measures productivity, in this book, we will also consider the health and happiness of employees. Without health or happiness, sustainability is totally unattainable.

It is no secret that depression, fatigue, and burnout of the workforce inhibits productivity, but factor in sick days and health crises for stressed out employees and you'll notice that these issues become huge financial burdens for the employer. The World

Health Organization (WHO) estimates that depression and anxiety cost the global economy $1 *trillion* dollars in lost productivity every year[3].

The pandemic, with its increase of home-office and remote work, caused an additional spike in this trend: In a study conducted by Indeed, over half of the respondents—52%—reported experiencing burnout. Not only is that every second worker: This is a significant overall increase compared to the 43% burnout recorded in the same study before COVID-19, just one year earlier[4]. From this sudden increase, we see just how dire the situation is. Cinderella's time is running out. Our clock reads 5 minutes to midnight. And in this case, Cinderella represents both our mental and physical health. So, what do we need to do before the clock strikes 12:00 am? Well, a few things.

Learning to Leverage Remote Opportunities

What if instead of adding to the problem of an already taxed health system, we could decrease the burden and utilize the benefits involved in the new era of remote work? And what if we could leverage positive benefits for both the employer and employee? We can, with long-term productivity in mind, as long as we acknowledge and avoid the short-term gains that have subsequent downfalls.

If we look at the information about remote work

before the pandemic, we will see that it was already on the rise. As early as 2007, in his book *The 4-Hour Workweek*, Timothy Ferriss proposes a version of working where one acts as a radical, digital nomad. The "character" in his book escapes the cubicle, finds a new business opportunity online, and logs on for work from a tropical destination. Although this was a wild concept in 2007 that only a few seemed to put into action, the advancement of both communication and technology has given rise to better, more numerous remote working opportunities.

This means the idea that you actually have to show up to work in your cubicle to be productive is fading. The worldwide governments enforced lockdowns and contact restrictions to protect people against a contagious virus. As a result, remote opportunities increased, with meetings and work-task completion through online software in virtual spaces becoming more necessary than ever. Now, even though lockdowns have ceased, the popularity of working this way remains.

The question we must ask, as remote work is still developing past its infancy, is: How can we use this helpful method sustainably?

A Note to Entrepreneurs

To all my friends who own their own businesses or consider themselves to be self-employed: I have a special message for you. The best analogy I've ever heard for entrepreneurs is by Toby Thomas, CEO of EnSuite Solutions. He says that the entrepreneur is like a person riding on top of a lion. The onlookers (which he says are regular employees or friends) feel a mix of sheer awe and envy for the lion-tamer and think "That person has everything together. Look at them riding the lion. They're so brave!" The person on the lion's back, however, is thinking "How the hell did I get here? And how do I keep myself from falling off and getting eaten?"

I know that feeling because I've been there. I know you probably have been too, whether you are 1 month or 5 years into riding the lion. In order to tame the beast and keep from falling and becoming lunch, entrepreneurs usually work harder than most. This is why hustle culture is most likely to pop up in their lives.

Motivational lines like "Grind now, shine later," "Late nights, early mornings," "I'd rather hustle 24/7 than be a slave to the 9-to-5," and "The road to success is always under construction," are enough to make entrepreneurs feel like outliers if they do anything but work their butts off 7 days a week. With all that in mind, I'm sure it won't come as a surprise to you that entrepreneurs are at an even higher risk of burning out than employees[5].

The problem is, in all the hustling, nobody talks about working smarter and making the hours count.

And the truth is, nobody needs true productivity as much as entrepreneurs do. When you own your own business, true productivity means being able to bill hours or sell products to your customers or clients instead of being caught up in busywork that does not yield revenue. And then, when you decide to take a vacation, usually no money comes in—so why bother going away at all?

Entrepreneurs also must make sure that they can keep coming up with the ideas and problem-solutions that their ever-changing entrepreneurship needs. They wear both hats: That of the inventor genius and that of the worker. In a one-person show, that person often finds themselves responsible for a multitude of different tasks and it becomes difficult to see what is busywork, and what work really creates active growth or progress. This ties into sustainability. Entrepreneurs must pay even closer attention to what they can sustain, since they are doing so much inside the business themselves.

Demands of the Future

When we're thinking about sustainability and remote work, there is a piece of the puzzle that a lot of people leave out: generational shifts. As the workforce matures and older generations age out, new generations with different values come in.

In the near future, companies will face changing

employee demands as the idea of what a good workplace is transforms according to what these younger generations value. Over the next few years, Millennials (those born between 1981 and 1996) and Generation Z (those born between 1997 and the late 2010s) will make up more and more of the workforce. Studies show that Millennials prioritize their work-life balance and flexible working hours over financial rewards[6]. Gone are the times when workers were willing to sell a bigger part of their free time if it meant they could secure a job with a well-established corporation with pensions and benefits.

It could be that the biggest driver of this shift will be Generation Z, who by 2025 will make up 27% of the workforce[7]. Generation Z's expectations when it comes to jobs and roles are highly value-driven and they seek to align their careers with their personal morals[8]. They will not only choose their workplaces in terms of what they can get for their time. They want value fits between them and their future employers.

If the values of the employee are their health and family time, they will look for companies that put processes and protocols into place that support those values. The times of telling, not showing, are over for employers. It's no longer going to be enough for companies to create copy that describes the work-life balance of their employees on a pretty website. Potential employees want to know what systems are in place to make that balance possible.

To keep up with these changes and continue to attract and retain talent, companies will have to rethink their work environments as well as the way job roles and fringe benefits are designed. Sustainability is a vital consideration to younger generations who are tired of hustle culture and the health compromises it demands.

A Sustainable Solution

To harness the full power of the changes we see happening in workplaces everywhere instead of being mere bystanders, there are models we need to rethink. As I learned, through the process of elimination the 3/2 workweek can create better productivity, lasting sustainability, and therefore better long-term health. Resilient employees are happier, keeping the churn rates and health costs for the employers low. It's a win-win system for a few reasons.

The 3/2 workweek fosters high quality working hours and adds to a balanced life while promoting happiness and preventing burnout. That is the reason I wrote this book: I know there are people out there who are looking for a better, more fulfilling, and healthier way to live. Throughout the rest of our journey together, I will help you understand why this system works, how it works, and what it can do for you personally.

The truth is, by working less, not only will you

naturally be more productive, you will also find that your life in general is more satisfying. It is also valuable to explore why it should be the employer's goal to focus on what can get done sustainably—independent of the number of hours logged by employees and whether those hours happen within a traditional 5 days on, 2 days off (5/2) workweek.

At first, my system might seem counterintuitive, but it's time to rethink the workweek and have a painfully honest look at not only how many hours we work, but the true output of that hourly investment. It's time to get more out of fewer hours. It's time to have happier, more dedicated employees that enjoy a healthy work-life balance over the next century. And it's time to start admitting that it's worth the effort to embrace a more sustainable work solution.

Key Takeaways

- True productivity is not adding more hours. It's adding higher quality work within the hours you have.
- In the past, our societies failed to look at the long-term effects of longer working hours on the health of employees, and it's time to change that.
- The pandemic opened the gateway to remote work, but no one has really taken the time to look at how we can use the advantages of working remotely while avoiding the pitfalls.

- The 9-to-5 in-person office setting will continue to become more and more outdated as new generations with different values enter the workforce.
- The goal of the 3/2 workweek is simple. For employees, it's to get more done and work fewer hours to enjoy what really matters in life. For employers, it's to keep employees engaged and healthy in the long run to avoid extensive turnover and health-care expenses.

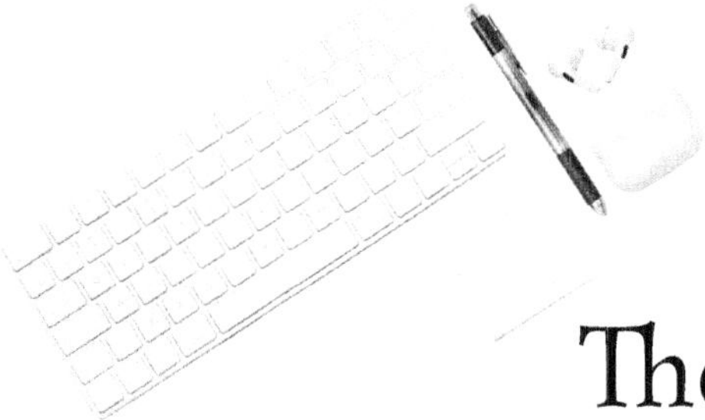

CHAPTER 3

The History of the 5 on, 2 off (5/2) Workweek

Even Henry Ford, over 100 years ago, realized that time off is not lost time or a class-based privilege.

To better understand where the 5/2 workweek (that averages 40 hours) came from, we need to look at how our working hours and the demands of the labor force developed over the previous thousands of years. Let's start at the beginning, when we were nomad cave-dwellers roaming the lands in small tribes. Most of us imagine the stone-age lifestyle as having to fight hand and tooth for everything. But was that really the case?

We think there was a ton to do back then just to survive, and the work required to stay alive must have been grueling. But here's the truth: Our ancestors got a lot more leisure time and had more freedom when choosing how to spend their working hours. Studies suggest that our hunting and foraging ancestors spent only around 20 hours per week working[9].

That breaks down to working 3 to 5 hours a day—which could vary greatly depending on the season or what needed to be done to survive. It's also important to mention that hunter and gatherer societies didn't have to invest time or effort in growing food, only finding it. With crop tending added into the equation, the hours needed to work per week increased to 30 hours, with the child-caring women taking more of that spike than the men[Ibid].

The number of hours worked continued to increase steadily over the next few centuries, mostly tied to the presence of sunlight. It seemed to have spiked during the summer in Medieval Times where dawn to dusk spanned a window of 16 hours during summer (in contrast to only 8 hours during winter). But even then, the working hours of a medieval peasant can't be compared with a modern middle-management worker.

The tempo of the so-called peasant was set to include both work and leisure, including frequent breaks for midmorning and midafternoon snacks. Naps were frequent[10]. Can you imagine taking a nap in the middle of the day at work? That would be amazing.

In fact, in those times, they usually didn't work more than 8 hours a day. With no rush to get things done and an abundance of leisure, many cultures were used to taking time off for holidays, saint's days, and other occasions like weddings or funerals (both of those being weekly celebrations, not the one- to two-day events we have nowadays). This adds up: In England, about a third of the year was spent without work. In ancient France, they had about 180 days off. And in Spain, they spent 5 months not working[Ibid]. It seems like while the workers were sometimes physically present for long hours (sunlight permitting), they were still not working full-time.

It wasn't until the Industrial Revolution that work hours per week spiked to a whopping 100 hours: gruesome 6-day weeks with 10 to 16 hours of daily work[11]. During this shift, the nature of how working hours were spent also changed drastically as society entered the machine age. The tempo of work became largely dictated by the speed of the assembly line. In addition to changes in ways people worked, there was also a unique technological development that made the shifts in the workweek even more dramatic.

With the invention of electric light in 1802, the days when dawn and dusk naturally regulated the working hours were gone. For investors, any time the machines were not running was time when they weren't increasing their profits. And with light during the night hours, that meant all 24 hours in a day could be filled with work. The owners of assembly lines didn't care if it was Sunday or a local saint's holiday.

Their factory was either running and making them money, or not. And they viewed the maintenance and break-down times as enough of an inconvenient loss of working time so time off was totally out of the question.

Transitioning From 100-Hour Workweeks to 40-Hour Workweeks

What business owners soon found, however, was that more hours did not necessarily mean more productivity or better work—especially when sick days, accidents, or assembly-line breakdowns caused by worker fatigue were taken into consideration. When they realized this, both industrial companies and labor unions alike started pushing for shorter working weeks around the turn of the 20th century.

The first attempt to limit working hours dates back to 1866, when the newly formed National Labor Union asked the United States Congress to mandate an 8-hour workday[12]. In subsequent years, the automobile producer, Henry Ford, ran 12 years of productivity experiments in his factories. The results of those studies led to the invention of the 5/2 workweek model, with 5 days working and 2 days off. Ford pioneered the 5/2 workweek almost 100 years ago in 1926, before it was common practice or mandated by law.

At that time in history, when the methods of the industrial revolution had normalized an average

100-hour workweek, Ford's method was considered revolutionary. There was immense backlash, but Ford stood by his results and answered his critics by noting that, in the same way the 8-hour workday created greater prosperity in America, the 5/2 workweek would create even more prosperity. He also noted that it was wrong to assume that off-time was a class privilege[13]. With the 5/2 workweek model, the Monday through Friday work schedule was born.

A Significant Change

Even though the average manufacturing employee worked 100 hours, 6 days a week, the productivity (as proven by Ford's experiments) was higher when the week was shortened to 40 hours total and broken down into 5 days, each containing 8 hours' worth of work. The revolution that Ford started was followed by a few other industrialists, but it took time to increase in popularity. It also took steady lobbying for the United States Congress to pass legislation in favor of the 40-hour workweek, which didn't happen until 1940[14].

The problem is that since 1940, the way we work hasn't changed. It's still the same 40 hours every workweek. Meanwhile, consider how much other things have changed in the same time: In 1940, out of 100 people, 2 owned cars[15]. The first public telephone had just come out (the one with rotary dial) and so had the black-and-white television.

Today, anyone reading this has both a phone and a television in their pocket in the form of a smartphone. Yet we still work the same 40-hour, 5-day rhythm Henry Ford invented 100 years ago. Weekly contractual hours are typical and only vary a small amount across different countries. The average working hours per week in the European Union between 2008 and the end of 2019 was 41 hours[16]. The United States leaves it up to the employer to set the contractual hours—but the U.S. Department of Labor guidelines provide overtime pay for more than 40-hour workweeks for non-exempt employees. The belief that longer hours means more productivity is deep-rooted through our working history and has held on long after Henry Ford proved that the truth is actually otherwise.

Time to Reframe— 40 *Contractual* Hours Usually Equate to 60 *Actual* Hours

At my first job after university, I learned about the big lie of the 40-hour workweek firsthand. You see, my contract stated that I needed to work exactly 42 hours. My workday started at 7:30am. If I went home before 7:00pm, I was one of the employees to leave the earliest. The higher up the ladder people were, the more hours employees spent at their desks. Friday was the big exception: We only worked until 5:00pm (insert my tiny jump for joy here). Not including our lunch break, this brought me to an average working week of around 51 hours.

I usually accumulated the 42 contractual hours by Thursday evening. I made a habit out of celebrating that accomplishment with a short coffee break and a big pat on my own back—and frequently a special post on Facebook or Twitter. Honestly, I was proud when my job placed new and sudden demands on me, or we were understaffed and I had to pitch in to do someone else's work. I would take to social media on Wednesday night and type "I am now starting the non-contractual hours for this week. Woohoo!"

I didn't question why we were all churning out these extra hours when the company couldn't legally require us to. And even though my total work hours were accomplished by Wednesday, I still worked the entire Thursday and Friday. In my mind, I was an extra special employee because I never took sick days or missed work on purpose.

The truth is, though, that I wasn't the only one who bought into the lies that hustle culture tells employees everywhere. The laws say one thing, but the reality of what people experience in the workplace is totally different. This is especially valid when you are in a mid- to high-level position.

Not only is it expected that you will work more than your 40-hour workweek, but you should expect to double it as 60 hours climbs higher to 80 or 100 hours per week. (Does 100 hours sound familiar? Yes, you're right. It's back to where it was during the industrial revolution.)

Behind these unspoken arrangements is the modus vivendi that if you want to get a high-ranking position, you need to work a lot. No matter what your contract says about how many hours you are paid for, the real working hours being logged have increased across all jobs in the last few decades. A study by Kuhn and Lonzano[17] showed that the percentage of American men regularly working more than 48 hours a week rose from 15.4% in the 1970s to 24.3% in 2005. And with higher income, the hours increased to about 80 hours per week: 62% of the high-earning individuals worked more than 50 hours a week, 35% more than 60 hours a week, and 10% worked more than 80 hours a week[18].

So, where does that leave us when we say "40-hour workweek"? Or someone has the audacity to put it in a contract? Few jobs still have an actual device to record hours worked—and the jobs that tend to create the highest overtime are often allowed to ignore this subject. It would go beyond the scope and goal of this book to pinpoint who is to blame or how to suggest a way to prevent this. But it is important for us to remember that when we speak about the 5/2 workweek, it is rarely just 40-hour workweeks we're discussing.

Time to Reframe—Remote Work Automatically Equals Fewer Work Hours Per Week

To say that the global COVID-19 pandemic disrupted life and the working environment substantially is not an overexaggeration. Most of the world went into shelter-at-home behavior between the middle of March and the middle of April in 2020. While initially, the hours worked per day shot up by a massive 2 to 3 hours per day[19], even after the pandemic, some of those extra hours hung around. A study comparing the workweeks before local lockdowns to the weeks after lockdowns showed that the workday had increased by 48.5 minutes, or 8.2%[20].

This will not be the last change the pandemic brings. Work will never go 100% back to the way it was before the pandemic. In many industries, what started as an unknown remote period has been expanded to almost 2 years. In fact, some companies are only partially going back to in-person offices. It is highly likely that in most industries, there will be some residual remote work as people create hybrid systems—whether due to a lasting pandemic or the restructuring that the pandemic initially caused.

After seeing what can be done remotely and how many desks remote work could potentially save an employer (22% of the companies have reduced office space[21]), logging into work from home or another remote location seems to be a trend that will last. In the future, some employers might choose to save expenses by renting less office space with a plan to have a percentage of workers employed remotely.

Because of this shift, the remote work fan base will find themselves in a better bargaining position than they were pre-COVID, with opportunities to negotiate not having to show their faces every day at the office. In fact, 1 in 2 people said they would look for a new job if they were no longer allowed to work remotely for the company they are currently with[Ibid].

With all these trends and facts in mind, it is vital for us to keep longer hours (and unwanted leaked-through hours) out of our free time when working remotely. One of the biggest challenges of remote work is the lack of physical or geographical boundaries. It used to be that the commute to work established those boundaries clearly. The car or train ride in to work equipped employees with an opportunity to mentally log in or out as they transitioned from home to work and vice versa. In remote environments, these boundaries are gone.

Feel the need to shoot off a quick email after the kids have gone to bed? No problem. Want to finish those slides for Tuesday's presentation on Sunday morning while your spouse is on the phone with a friend? It's just a click away. What seems to be an amenity (freely choosing when to work) takes away much needed downtime that would naturally be blocked off due to the geography of an in-person workplace. It is also worth mentioning that these at-home behaviors are now supported by the increase of portable technology. For remote workers of the 21st century, there is no natural dividing line.

Always "being on" and "just a log-in away from work" is not an optimal situation for recovery. It doesn't provide a good environment for free time or a thorough recharge. When working from home, there need to be alternatives so that employees can reestablish boundaries that jobs with regular commutes would bring—to limit the total working hours to a reasonable, decent number. But what is a decent number of hours to work? Is there a sweet spot between our natural ability to concentrate and perform and the hours needed to ensure our work gets done? And do certain types of labor lend themselves to needing longer or shorter hours?

How Many Hours Should We Really Work?

When we're thinking about how many hours we put in at work, we always need to be asking this big question: How long can I sustain my ideal level of productivity through these accumulating hours? This question leads us to a second one. How do the productivity studies run by Henry Ford apply to our modern age?

Think about today's average employee—the middle

manager and the manager above them. If they are pushing past the 60-hour workweek, are they really more productive than those assembly workers who Ford proved weren't efficient anymore at that same point? To understand how to answer that question, we need to think about the last 100 years. Has that much really changed? Should we work more or fewer hours to improve productivity? Or is 60 hours per workweek a good number? These are all questions we have to answer before we can be certain our solutions for long-term working strategies will succeed.

Thursdays were always a drag back before my 3/2 workweeks. While Mondays and Tuesdays in the 5/2 model felt good and I felt productive, by Thursday, I felt like I was running on empty—no matter how much coffee I drank or how many breaks I took. Determined to fix my productivity problem, I went through piles of self-help books in an effort to find out how to refill my tank halfway through the week.

So, I experimented with what the books told me. For example, I got up and started even earlier in the morning to take advantage of the quiet hours when I could be super productive. But then my afternoon slump hit earlier. The results I wanted eluded me.

The question that kept running through my head was "How can I get more out of the week?" I tried working longer on the good days: Monday and Tuesday. I tried planning bigger breaks later in the week or a shorter day on Wednesday. But nothing changed: By the end of the week, I was dragging my feet at best.

Here and there I still had hope that a short Facebook scrolling break would get me through to the 5:00pm bell (or whatever the earliest socially-acceptable time was to leave the workplace). That never worked. No matter what I did, there seemed to be a magic line somewhere after the first 25 to 30 hours of work where my productivity, drive, energy, and motivation dropped off in dramatic fashion (I see that clearly now, then, not so much).

The current hustle narrative is that with the less backbreaking work of our modern age, more hours must equal more work done: since mind power is all that is required for many office jobs. This is why it doesn't come as a surprise to us that ambitious employees are regularly seen putting in extra hours. Even though it is illegal not to pay employees for overtime being worked, many manager contracts specifically exempt overtime pay. It's that much of a standard managerial approach. So much so, that no employee questions this clause in their contract.

Time to Reframe—More Doesn't Always Mean More When It Comes to Work Hours

More time at work (whether physical or remote) is generally seen as a way to get more done. But as you'll discover in this section of the book, quite the opposite is true.

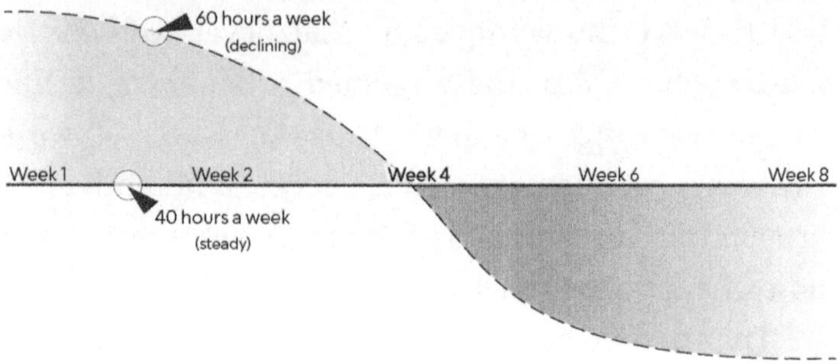

Graphing Productivity and Overtime

In the graph above, you can see that the productivity spike in a 60-hour workweek is short-lived[22]. While there is an initial jump in the amount of work getting accomplished in the first 2 weeks, the positive effect is reversed past the 4-week mark.

Going back to our racing horse example, the flogged horse will initially speed up and go faster—but after the third sprint, its energy is spent. In fact, the animal's energy is spent past the point it was at when it started the training regime. And for our worker on the graph, the buildup of fatigue caused by the surplus hours reduces the average productivity so that it falls below the steady state of what we see at 40 hours per week. While it might initially seem like a spike in productivity to work additional hours, this is reversed in the long run as productivity tanks. And we still need to answer the question "Does less physical labor mean we can be more productive with added hours?"

Time to Reframe—Creative Problem-Solving Doesn't Need Special Consideration in Relation to Productivity

Personally, I'm always interested in how creative people work. As a problem-solver myself, I'm also curious about how this specific skill relates to productivity. Studies show that creativity and the ability to problem-solve effectively decreases even faster than other types of work. Fatigue is more significant with these tasks than it is with manual labor. The performance for knowledge workers declines after just 35 hours, as opposed to 40 hours[Ibid].

This presents us with compelling evidence that we should examine the 100-year-old, 40-hour workweek with more scrutiny. When compared to the Industrial Age, a substantial part of how we work has switched from factory belt to computer. And often, these days, the tasks have shifted toward creative ones.

Today's world relies on the creativity of our present workforce for future innovation (which also translates to sales). That is why measuring employees solely based on their present productivity falls short. Employees need time to explore creative solutions. And if employers and companies try to squeeze every ounce of productivity out of the employee's working time, creativity cannot flourish—and with a desertion of creativity, society is also giving up future products and sales opportunities.

Google was one of the first companies to notice this problem and established a policy to actively encourage their employees to spend 20% of their time on non-work-related side projects. By effectively allowing them to spend one full workday a week on something that isn't related to current work projects, they made space for future innovations and creative endeavors. Other companies, inspired by Google, have also adopted this approach after seeing the amazing results of Google's experiment: Products like Gmail, Google Maps, Twitter, Slack, and Groupon all started as side projects. If you ever had a solution to a work-related problem hit you on your day off, or while helping your kid on their science project, you have experienced this effect too.

And now that we've looked at how different approaches to time spent create different results, let's talk about how different days of the week have to be evaluated individually as well.

Time to Reframe—Productivity Is the Same Monday Through Friday

If you've ever worked with a 5/2 workweek schedule, it is no secret to you that your productivity at the beginning of the week is at a different level than it is on Friday. Whether that reason has more to do with how refreshed you're feeling after time off or the optimism that greets you in the new week, you probably still feel like you're getting more done on Monday than you are on Friday. The truth is, you are.

The project management tool company, Redbooth, wanted to know the actual numbers behind that feeling, and discovered that what gets done on Monday versus what we accomplish on Friday is displayed in numbers as an 18% drop in productivity[23]. That is a significant percentage. This means that every 5th hour you work on Friday is spent accomplishing nothing when compared to Monday.

It's an industry-wide secret in marketing that you don't send out newsletters on Friday. People are less likely to have the energy or time to read them, so the risk that they get lost among other emails in an overflowing inbox and forgotten is significant. This is why the preference is to target email subscribers sometime between Monday and Wednesday, when they're more likely to open those messages. Generally, Tuesday is the favorite day to send out newsletters.

When looking at the productivity that occurs Monday through Wednesday, we notice it is fairly high and consistent. Tuesday falls in productivity by only 1%, while on Wednesday we tend only to be 5% less productive than on Monday. It is not until Thursday (with a 9% drop compared to Monday) that the difference becomes more substantial[Ibid].

As we work our way through these studies and details, a clear pattern seems to be emerging.

Time to Reframe—Hours Worked Predict Levels of Productivity: As Revealed by GDPs Everywhere

To get an idea of productivity across different workweek totals, let's have a look at statistics from different countries. The number of contractual hours worked per week differs across the globe. But does an increase in work hours result in more productivity? In the past, the assumption was "yes." But if that assumption was correct, the output generated by the countries with higher working hours would be significantly higher than the output of the countries with fewer working hours. How can we measure country-wide productivity? There's one number we can definitely take into consideration.

The most generally accepted number to measure productivity for large-scale entities like countries is the gross domestic product, also referred to as the GDP. With that in mind, let's take a look at a chart that takes the GDP and average working hours for 2019 into consideration. (2019 is a good year to look at because the pandemic didn't affect working hours.)

The Organisation for Economic Co-operation and Development (OCED) has collected numbers that show that more hours per workweek don't result in higher levels of productivity[24]. As you can see in the chart below, Denmark has the lowest annual working hours in the world, and their GDP per hour is among the highest, claiming spot number 4. And Denmark is in good company as 8 of the countries that rank in the top 10 for GDP also rank in the top 13 countries for fewest working hours. On this list of top 10, only Ireland and the United States rank over 25 in the column that indicates higher working hours.

Ranking of GDP (2019)	Country	Average hours worked per person employed	Rank lowest to highest in working hours
1	Ireland	1771.2	30
2	Luxembourg	1506.7	7
3	Norway	1381.6	2
4	Denmark	1371.5	1
5	Switzerland	1549.4	12
6	Belgium	1577.0	13
7	United States	1741.2	25
8	Sweden	1452.0	5
9	Austria	1509	8
10	Netherlands	1438.5	4

When we consider the data, higher work hours do not seem to be an intrinsic indicator of a higher GDP: they are inversely linked. The number of hours worked does not actually guarantee a high GDP.

To further undermine the idea that more hours automatically equal more productivity, let's think about the other side of this scale in terms of most hours worked. If what hustle culture tells us is true, those who have the highest hours of work should have the highest GDPs.

If we think about the opposite end of the scale, Colombia, Mexico, Korea, Costa Rica, Malta, and Russia are rated in the top 6 of the most hours worked[Ibid]. But they come in at an average place of 60 on the GDP per Capita ranking for 2019. As we look at this side of the scale, the data still doesn't give us evidence that more work hours correlate with productivity.

Throughout the course of history, the hours worked per week has fluctuated, driven by either the demands of the work that needed to be performed or by the demands of employers. It was only in the Industrial Age that people became interested in intentionally testing the total work hours to see what number would be ideal for productivity.

Since Henry Ford paved the way for this kind of research 100 years ago, few have thought about the actual best numbers for working hours and the related maximum and minimum productivity output in today's workplace. We know, based on the graph we saw in this chapter, that the assumption that 60-hour workweeks spike long-term in productivity has been disproven. The initial productivity spike drops below the 40-hour workweek average after a short time. Looking at the standard measures for productivity, GDP, and hours worked brings us to another revelation.

Looking at the working hours in contrast to the GDP outputs of different countries shows us that there isn't a link between working more and being more productive. In fact, it's quite the opposite: we find a lot of countries with lower work hours perform well as far as country GDP. So, while more time at work does seem positive in concept because it feels like there should be greater output, the evidence is not there to support that feeling. It's time for us to look more critically at the situation to determine if there are more negative aspects to working longer hours than there are positive ones. Especially now that we know the spike of productivity isn't there.

Key Takeaways

- Over the centuries, people worked longer and longer hours. Historically, we went from 20 hours a week of work in the Stone Age to 100 hours over 6 days in the Industrial Age.
- Henry Ford ran productivity experiments which resulted in a 5/2 workweek with 40 hours. This is still the model most use today.
- Most often, contracted 40-hour workweeks end up as workweeks with 60+ hours.
- Our productivity declines when we work more hours.
- For both creative and problem-solving work, 35 hours a week is the sweet spot.
- The number of hours we work does not correlate directly with productivity. On the contrary, countries with fewer working hours consistently place high as far as GDP.

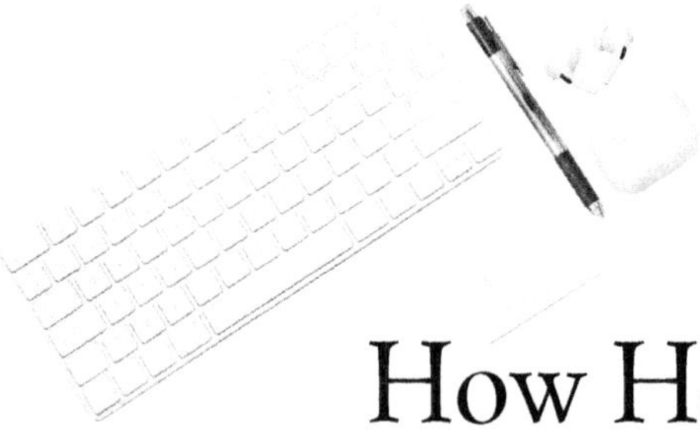

CHAPTER 4

How Health and Happiness Are Linked to Work Hours

If you keep putting in 8-hour days, you may eventually level up to be a boss who works 12-hour days.

Entrepreneurship is great, right? You get to do your own thing, be your own boss. Ride the lion! Until your job, the one you created, becomes your new boss. On my own entrepreneurial journey, that boss was like a beeping alarm, attempting wildly to drag me out of my dreams, and I hated it. I hadn't signed up to need a 4:30 am alarm clock that would yell me awake to go to work. Why was I doing that to myself?

Over 6 years into this "running my own business" dream gig, the excitement was gone. Remember the last time you fell head over heels in love? The first you thought about in the morning was your crush. The last thing you thought before you fell asleep was your crush. Right? That's what my first couple of years of entrepreneurship had been like.

I hadn't paid myself a dime the first few years because it was "just a passion." The sheer excitement of being able to do it was better than getting paid. Remember when you didn't care where you went for your date, as long as you got to spend time with the person you loved? That was back when every single moment with your date was great. Maybe they made noises when they chewed their food, but you gently overlooked that fact because you were so happy to be with them.

My honeymoon phase with my business was definitely over 6 years in. And the first 5 minutes of each day showed how my story had changed in dramatic fashion. It was no longer a fairy tale. In a semi-conscious state right after that dreaded alarm went off, I hated everything. I had to use extreme motivation just to get myself moving.

My pre-rehearsed lines usually started with "You are the one opening the doors today. Your clients count on you," and "The early class is one of the most popular." Then I would try to remind myself why this was my passion in the first place. "You like coaching!" or "You love this job, remember?"

Deep down, though, I remembered how it had started. I used to jump out of bed and couldn't contain my excitement. Now all I could think of were the problems. It was like I just noticed that my date always chewed their food soooo loudly, and I was annoyed that this one thing ruined the whole dinner-date experience!

Everything in my business had become a chore. Everything I did was rushed and last minute when I had used to plan things ahead. Now, I either didn't have time, or when I had time and free space on my morning calendar, I wouldn't be able to drag myself out of bed to do anything.

I used to go out looking for new opportunities, ideas, events, and business opportunities. Now, if it wasn't essential to running the business or putting out the metaphorical fires that popped up daily, I couldn't muster the energy to bother.

I figured it was just a slump. I figured I just hadn't stomached the most recent crisis yet (and there were always crises, whether financial, staff-related, or due to yet another customer complaint). After the blood and sweat, this was definitely a tears phase. But was it just a phase? I was starting to suspect it was something more. I had quit my 9-to-5 career to build my dream job—but now all I had was a 24/7 job and a nightmare. To say I was unhappy would definitely be an understatement.

I tried to feel more abundant by hiring and empowering the right staff. But if that worked for some months (before another crisis came along), I was only putting more distance between what I had come to dread and myself, not actually changing my feelings. And even though I felt miserable, I couldn't just quit.

The thing about entrepreneurship is that you become mentally invested. Your business can become your identity. There was simply no other option in my mind than to find a way to improve what I had. I assumed that if I could manage that, I could miraculously go back to being motivated. Have you ever been there?

It's hard to change paths if you have forged them, laid down strong foundations, and invested in seeing them succeed. I wanted so badly to make it work and see it through, but it wasn't working. I think at that point, I would've needed a metaphorical train to run into me to realize that—and the pandemic was the derailed train that would do just that.

Are you still in the honeymoon phase of your job? Excited to go to work—not bored by the 20-40% of stuff you don't really like doing? I'm asking because, at this point in my story, something started happening with more frequency. I started to feel sick. I started to get sick. And when I thought about how much I had gotten sick before I started my wild ride on the lion of entrepreneurship, I noticed a huge difference. So, here's a question I want you to consider: How often did you use to get sick—and how often do you get sick now?

Time to Reframe—It's Impossible for Our Work to Affect Our Health

There is a growing body of research that shows us a worrisome trend: there are links between long working hours and the health issues of workers. What Henry Ford realized 100 years ago still holds true today: Working long hours has direct implications on health by increasing fatigue-related injuries. But there are other work-related health issues to be concerned about than just direct work injuries.

In one study, working overtime was associated with a 61% higher injury rate when compared to jobs without overtime. This rate was at 37% for days with 12+ hours and at 23% for weeks with 60+ hours[25]. But to think that this is an issue only the assembly line or construction worker deals with is a mistake. The increase was neither linked to the industry of work nor the number of hours (the thought being that more hours worked equaled more hours of exposure). The cause was pure overwork.

So, it doesn't even matter if it's a night shift or a seemingly riskier job like cleaning the windows of a skyscraper or operating large machinery. Desk workers are at the same risk for injuries after a long day.

Now that you see the adverse effects that long working hours have on health (no matter what kind of work the position entails), let's look at the scarier, less logical ones. In no particular order, here we go—for the sake of better informed choices, we must enter the cabinet of horrors:

Heart Attacks

A study by the World Health Organization (WHO) shows that between the years 2000 and 2016, the numbers of ischemic heart disease deaths attributable to working 55+ hours increased by a whopping 41.5%. In the year 2016, a total of over 398,000 stroke deaths were caused by exposure to long working hours[26].

Type 2 Diabetes

Working overtime at a level of more than 12 hours a week has been shown to increase the likelihood of Type 2 Diabetes by 370%[27].

Depression, Unhealthy Weight Gain, and/or Increase in Smoking

The more we work, the more it seems to dampen our spirits, often urging us to seek refuge in comfort foods or drugs: Long hours have been linked to depression, unhealthy weight gain, and an increase in smoking[28].

Alcoholism

People who work long hours (more than 48) are 12% more likely to become heavy drinkers in comparison to those who work standard hours (35-40) per week[29].

Burnout

Workweeks longer than 40 hours are linked to increased risk for burnouts with even higher risk as workers hit 60+ hours. Plus, the likelihood of burnout is even higher for employees younger than 50 years old, women, and those who are physically inactive[30].

Death

In Japan, overwork and its strain on health is such a prevalent issue, there is a Japanese term for it. *Karoshi* literally means "death by overwork," and is an official term listed as one cause of death in Japan's health statistics. It first appeared after the 1973 oil crisis—when reports emerged of people literally dropping dead at their workplaces. Another type of *karoshi* happens when people are so stressed about workplace issues that they commit suicide. Since 1973, it has not improved: In 2019, according to Japanese Government statistics, almost 10% of the suicides were related to work[31]. Let's take a stab in the dark and assume this rate will not decrease in the 2020-era with its unique challenges.

This list is by no means complete—and for every risk factor, the studies continue to pile up.

Time to Reframe—High Happiness Can't Possibly Be Directly Linked to Fewer Work Hours

Now that we've looked at how illnesses are linked to overwork, let's look at its link to happiness—or the lack of happiness when it comes to productivity and long work hours.

The same way that countries are ranked by hours spent working and GDP, there is also a happiness ranking. This happiness report that comes out every year is based largely on the Gallup World poll where citizens are asked to give a happiness score from 1 to 10. What has been a constant over recent years is that Nordic countries like Finland, Denmark, Norway, Sweden, and Iceland have ranked in the Top 8 of the Worldwide Happiness ranking every year from 2018 to 2022[32].

	2018	2019	2020	2021	2022
1	**Finland**	**Finland**	**Finland**	**Finland**	**Finland**
2	**Denmark**	**Denmark**	**Denmark**	**Denmark**	**Denmark**
3	**Norway**	**Norway**	Switzerland	Switzerland	**Iceland**
4	**Iceland**	**Iceland**	**Iceland**	**Iceland**	Switzerland
5	New Zealand	Netherlands	**Norway**	Netherlands	Netherlands
6	Australia	Switzerland	Netherlands	**Norway**	Luxembourg
7	Canada	**Sweden**	**Sweden**	**Sweden**	**Sweden**
8	**Sweden**	New Zealand	New Zealand	Luxembourg	**Norway**

World Happiness Ranking 2018-2022
(Nordic Countries in Bold)

While there have been many reasons named and further explored for this trend in happiness ranking, what is striking is that when looked at next to countries that have the fewest work hours, many of the top 11 of show up with the highest happiness rankings as well.

Furthermore, if we then look at GDP, the happy Nordic countries also place in the top 14 around the world. Let's take a look.

	Happiness Rank (2019)	GDP Ranking (2019)	Hours Worked Ranking (Low to high)
Finland	1	14	11
Denmark	2	4	1
Norway	3	3	2
Iceland	4	13	6
Netherlands	5	10	4
Switzerland	6	5	12
Sweden	7	8	5
New Zealand	8	27	33
Canada	9	18	21
Austria	10	9	8

Happiness, GDP, and Work-Hour Ranking Comparison

Five countries show up in all 3 categories of the different top 10 lists for happiness, highest GDP, and the fewest working hours: Denmark, Norway, Netherlands, Sweden, and Austria. An astonishing 8 out of the 10 of the happiest countries also score in the top 14 for GDP as well as the top 12 for the fewest hours worked around the world[33]. Have we found the secret trifecta?

To find such a high correlation between happiness, high GDP, and low work hours does suggest a good work-life balance is possible: work less, be happier, and still reach the productivity targets (high GDP) of countries (or the companies in them). Talking about putting hope back into our lives!

Contrary to higher working hours being linked to higher productivity, which we disproved in chapter 3, quite the opposite seems to be happening. There even seems to be a golden triumvirate made of a high productivity (measured in GDP), fewer-than-average work hours, and a happy workforce population. It almost sounds too good to be true. Work less, get better results, and be happy. But is that really what's going on?

You Can't Vacation Your Way Out of Overwork

What about our annual leave? You know, vacation time. Surely a 2-week getaway will allow an overworked employee to rest and recover so they come back refreshed and ready to chip away at work again?

Think about the last time you went on vacation. Usually the last week before you leave peaks in stress. Why? You're trying to get everything at work done in time to leave. Then there's the packing. Cleaning out the fridge so nothing spoils. Not to mention all the little things you have yet to think of. The 3:00 am wake-up call on the departure day to catch the flight doesn't help either.

By the time you arrive at your destination, the

multiple layovers and delays have taken such a toll that you are ready to skip the punch part of the rum & punch welcome drink. It takes you a couple of days to truly unwind, and in the back of your head, you're still wondering if you locked the windows. Plus, you're worried that your boss will have questions for you while you're gone.

By the time you've fully switched off, it is time to go back. You're already dreading the overflowing inbox and are seriously considering logging in during your layover or the night before you go back to work, just to make sure you can get through all the emails.

Your first days back at the desk, you can still feast on those lovely memories of days spent with sand between your toes—your biggest worry being whether your swimsuit would dry in time for the next meal. But work has a way of bringing you back to reality and those relaxing days soon are forgotten.

If this sounds like you, you aren't alone. While vacations do improve health and well-being[34], according to research, it takes anywhere between 3 days and a couple of weeks for your stress levels to return back to what they were pre-vacation—even if you felt burned-out. This means you will go right back to how you felt before your vacation just 3 short weeks after it[35].

This all points to the fact that while vacations do offer good respite and rest from work, a single event (or even 2 events) can't be used to compensate for bad habits during the rest of the year. It's similar to sleep—you need to sleep daily. You cannot accumulate a sleep debt over a period of time and hope to make it up suddenly. So, we cannot rely on vacations alone to take the stress out of our work life and help us come back recovered.

Key Takeaways

- Working long hours is detrimental to one's health: Studies show working 40+ hours increases the risks of heart attacks, Type 2 diabetes, and depression.
- If we look at the world happiness ranking, there is a trifecta of the top-ranking countries: They work fewer hours while still having high GDPs. So, not only is it possible to work fewer hours and be productive, but it also makes us happier.
- Being healthy or relaxed is not something you can postpone until later in the year when you get those much needed 2 weeks off: The effect of a vacation wears off after a couple of weeks back at work.

CHAPTER 5

The Working World Is Changing

Your best ideas don't come to you during stressful situations. They usually come when you're under the water in the shower or falling asleep.

Now that we've seen how productivity needs to be measured in a different way based on the golden triumvirate we discussed in the last chapter, it's time to talk about another needed and wanted change. As the workforce itself changes, younger generations are not willing to simply put up with the strenuous work life of their parents in exchange for financial payment. The way they live is different, and it makes sense that they also want to see the way they work transform as well.

Time to Reframe—Millennials Are Wrong for Demanding a Better Work-Life Balance

The trend that people would rather opt for more free time than financial benefits started with Millennials[36], but will only increase with the older generation maturing out of the workforce. Generation Z is coming in. And a model with more free time, like the 3/2 workweek, would not only satisfy the updated demands of employees, but improve overall company performances as well.

Time to Reframe—Work Cannot Be More Asynchronous or Remote

In the industrial economy of the 1900s, the nature of work was synchronous. In synchronous work, you need someone else to complete steps 1 and 2 so you can do your work on steps 3 and 4. So, it made sense to have fixed workdays and the same work hours for everyone.

You can't run a vehicle assembly line if the employee bolting in the motor is not at work Wednesday and would rather come Sunday when everyone else is off. But the nature of our work today is becoming more and more what is referred to as asynchronous, where there is less need to wait for your colleague, the one ahead of you in line, to finish his work so you can do yours.

In an asynchronous working environment, each employee can perform the main body of their work without being dependent on other inputs. As a result, their timeline can be completely individual and distributed over days and weeks—their work time is flexible up until the final deadline where the work is delivered.

Asynchronous work does not rely on fixed Monday through Friday weeks or 9-to-5 schedules in shared office spaces. If you think your boss, company, or industry is different, here are some questions you can ask yourself to shift your perspective: Which services do you not perform at your workplace? Do you have your own lawyers in house—or do you hire a firm? Do you work with a marketing agency? How about the payroll, healthcare, or facility management? As you've probably already guessed, this type of work is asynchronous as well as remote (remote work is also referred to as outsourced or contracted work).

It seems likely that the synchronous jobs still left (like a cashier or forklift driver) will become more and more automated until humans are fully replaced by technology. Go to any medium-sized grocery store today. They will have a self-checkout system. In furniture stores, there are computer terminals where you can search the database for your question instead of asking an employee. Do you think that there are still a lot of human-dependent tactile jobs out there? Think again: There are even robots posing as baristas in fully automated coffee bars where you can get your coffee specialties on demand—complete with a poured coffee heart in your foam.

Wait, but what about customer service? Well, when was the last time you tried to get a real person on the phone? I recently tried to locate a package that I was sending to a friend. The online tracking code said the package had been stuck at a nearby distribution center for 7 days. I couldn't even find a phone number where I could reach a human anywhere on their website. Companies nowadays intentionally make it harder for you to reach a real person. Do you think this is by coincidence or by plan?

Traditional customer service options are being replaced by technology whenever and wherever possible. Technological developments and artificial intelligence are replacing customer interactions. For example, there are chatbots that answer client questions. A chatbot is an artificial intelligence that simulates human conversation through a live chat interface and learns from the interactions. Responses and keywords will be pre-programmed, and the chatbot can provide self-service solutions based on the analysis of each customer's chat. This is just the start of what this kind of technology can achieve. Juniper research estimates that 75% to 90% of queries are projected to be handled using bots by 2024[37].

Time to Reframe—The Bulk of the Work Has to Get Done at the Office

Ask asynchronous employees where they would go to get the most work done and they will answer that they would *not* go into the office—or if they would, it would be early, on weekends, or they would stay in late on a Friday after everyone has left. The truth about the last 20 years of office design development is that the nice open space, converging rooms, and break rooms with amenities have all created environments that are almost impossible to work in without interruption.

The moment you walk into the office, the distractions start. Your sales colleague calls. Betty stops by to ask about your weekend. The project manager quickly checks in to ask if you've heard from the client. Then, a co-worker's phone alert starts going off. Not to mention the bustling of the socializing in the break room that travels through the open office space. The number of distractions is too numerous to count.

On average, an office worker loses over 6 hours to interruption per day according to a Washington Post article by Brigid Schulte. According to Schulte: The interruptions make up a total of 238 minutes; refocusing costs another 84 minutes; and the errors, stress, and fatigue from the ordeal cost another 50 minutes[38]. So, if you're working your 10-hour day in the office, and have 3 hours' worth of meetings—that leaves you with 1 focused hour to get work done. It's no wonder that people wait until off hours to attempt doing their work at the office.

Time to Reframe—Remote Work Opportunities Will Eventually Go Away

The lasting effects of the global pandemic will undoubtedly cause many industries and social areas to change. But for remote work, there is no other single event that has had a bigger impact. With the flip of the switch in March 2020, even traditional companies had to rethink what could be done remotely.

With that in mind, it is important to note that remote work is nothing new: it was around long before the pandemic. In 2015, the level of freelancers (independent workers contracted for specific tasks who work in their own spaces) in America was 30%. The most extreme model of this was first presented to the wide public by Timothy Ferriss in his famous book *The 4-Hour Workweek*. We've previously discussed that in this book, Ferriss presented the digital nomad: an employee that logs on to work at anytime from anywhere in the world.

Since then, the improvements in technology (like cellular data transfer rates and improved cell phone coverage) have given rise to this segment of work. Predictions even prior to the impact of the pandemic guessed there would be 1 billion digital nomads by 2035[39]. But employees don't have to log in from

Thailand or their next stop along their world travels. Working remotely can mean you work for a company in a large city, but enjoy suburban life. In turn, for the employers, this means they can recruit from the best talent in the world and are not bound to the employees who live close by and they can also avoid having to offer moving assistance to incentivize workers with specific skills to relocate.

Remote work can be anything done remotely, which can include outsourced segments like human resources or legal. Remote also can refer to freelancers and independent contractors. The pandemic has put additional pressure on both companies and employees to admit that remote work is possible. Even if companies want to go back to the way things were before, if they want to move into the future, they will have to rethink remote work opportunities.

Time to Reframe—Remote Work Can't be More Productive or Collaborative Than Traditional Work—Or Make People Happier and Healthier

For years, there has been a debate over how productive you could be if you worked where you lived. We don't have to debate anymore—as the studies now show—productivity is higher at home than in the office. In a study done by Stanford's Graduate School of Business, over a period of 9 months, it was discovered that there was a 13% performance increase when working at home. Of which, 9% was attributed to fewer breaks and sick days, and 4% to a quieter work environment[40].

We also now know this is backed up by the subjective feeling of employees working remotely: Research by Owl Lab during the pandemic shows that with almost 70% of U.S. full-time workers logging in remotely, 90% of them say they were just as productive, if not more so[41]. And 22% were happier working from home[Ibid]. A study by Ergotron found that next to job satisfaction and work-life balance, the remote setting increased the physical health of the employees by 75%, and 56% of them even gained improvements in their mental health[42].

The second biggest argument employers usually have against remote work is that it makes teamwork and collaboration more difficult. But in a survey of 1,000 workers in a remote setting, 78% said they feel that remote work has improved the collaboration with colleagues at their organization[Ibid].

As dramatic as this change is, the way we work has still stayed the same for over 100 years, which proves that the time to adjust our thinking about the workplace is now, not later.

Key Takeaways

- The upcoming main force in our working population, the Millennials, would rather work less than earn more.
- The nature of our work is becoming more and more asynchronous—we don't have to wait on someone else to complete a task before we do or even be in the same room with them.
- Work is not getting done in our open space offices because there are too many distractions. On an average work day, you lose over 6 hours due to distractions and the refocusing and correcting time that comes as a result.
- Remote work opportunities have been around since the digital nomad showed up in Timothy Ferriss's book, *The 4-Hour Workweek*, in 2007—but the pandemic really lit a fire under the opportunities. From outsourced departments to freelance contractors, remote work can take different shapes and forms.
- Remote work is more productive and workers report they feel happier and strike a better work-life balance.

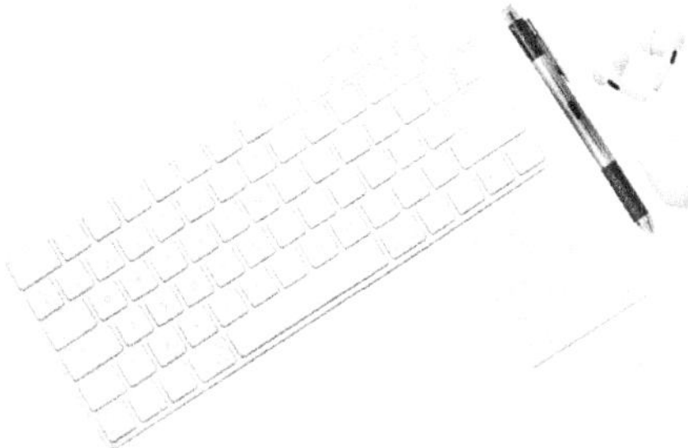

CHAPTER 6

The 4-Day Workweek and What It Teaches Us

If you keep postponing happiness, you might find yourself waking up one day and looking back on a life made solely of unhappy moments.

In the last chapter, we looked at how the demand of workers along with our technological advancements combined with the pandemic increased remote work and created an overall shift in approaches toward employment. Now, let's look at what employers have come up with to address those changes so far.

Time to Reframe—The 4-Day Workweek and the 5/2 Workweek in Terms of Productivity

Not all of the working world revolves around the 100-year-old model of the 5/2 workweek. There are trailblazers embarking into new models like a 4-day workweek. In March of 2018, Perpetual Guardian, a company in New Zealand, launched a groundbreaking trial and gave its employees an additional day off per week without decreasing pay. Every staff member worked a 4-day week, consisting of 30 hours, but got paid for the same 37.5 hours that used to be their contractual number in the 5/2 workweek model. The University of Auckland accompanied the trial, measured the outcome, and published the results.

They found that job performance was maintained even with the shorter week—showing that the amount of work achieved was the same[43]. Contrary to what you might first believe, this did not come with an increase of working hours per day. They achieved the measured results with business productivity guidelines that were defined before the trial. And during the study, it was emphasized to the staff that they should not work extra hours during their 4 days[Ibid].

Time to Reframe—4-Day Weeks, Stress and Burnouts

In the Perpetual Guardian study, not only did employee stress levels decrease, but team engagement improved across several measured areas like commitment (from 68% before to 88% after the trial), stimulation (from 66% to 84%) and empowerment (from 68% to 86%) [Ibid]. Is this a coincidence or a onetime fluke?

It doesn't seem to be a coincidence as more and more examples pile up: The country of Iceland implemented a 4-day week in their administration (which amounts to 1% of Iceland's total working population) and found similar results. Productivity remained the same. Worker well-being dramatically increased as seen by marked improvements in health and work-life balance and marked decreases in stress and burnout. The lead researcher, Haraldsson, said that the success of the shorter workweek for specific people in Iceland tells us that this method is a possibility for our modern times and that progressive change can happen[44].

Seeing that the productivity of the 5/2 workweek was matched in the shorter 4-day week is great information, but maybe the most important result was that those employees experienced less stress with this decrease of the total workdays and hours. The employees reported a pre-trial stress level of 45% and a post-trial level of 38%. In addition, employee agreement that the work-life balance was good improved from 54% to 78%[45].

Spoiler alert: Perpetual Guardian still works a 4-day workweek. The initial—well researched—experiment has been prolonged. If you are interested in learning more, I highly recommend reading *The 4 Day Week* by Andrew Barnes, the man who set this experiment in motion[46].

Since then, several companies have joined the

trend (Bolt, Uncharted, The Wanderlust Group) and Spain is piloting a 4-day workweek for companies, in part, due to the challenges of the Coronavirus. Unilever consumer goods company is completing a trial with staff in New Zealand, presenting them with an opportunity to cut their hours by 20% without the fewer hours impacting their pay.

The novelty of this concept is that there was not a trade-off between hours worked and amount of currency paid. Usually, working fewer days a week is reserved exclusively for part-time models hinging on the employees' requirements or desires to have more days off (for example, parents who need to be home to care for children).

A 4-day week would translate to an 80% part-time job, a transaction where the employer would essentially pay 20% less for 20% fewer working hours. But if we can prove that the same productivity can be accomplished in 4 days as it can in 5, shouldn't the 4-day workweek become the new norm? (And without the employees having to suffer a cut in pay?) What if we approached it with productivity in mind instead of just the number of hours worked?

Change Is Never Easy

As the initiative at Perpetual Guardian was launched, many employees were concerned about how they were going to get the same work done in less time.

In response, overtime was strictly prohibited. While the productivity measured well, the initial feedback did raise some concerns and uncover some anxiety. Change is never easy—even if it sounds perfect: Work less, get the same amount of work done, and get paid the same salary. Resisting change is part of being human. And I am not just talking about your boss, I'm talking about you too.

One might think, "It worked some 100 years and we're still here, so why change it?" I can hear your inner voice singing the tune. But don't forget: Our lizard brains are wired for survival. Survival in the primal times meant you stick to the berries you knew didn't kill you last week. Stay in the shelter that has a nearby creek that's never run dry. This fear of change is something that has caused me to question my options more than once. Let's take a look at one of those many times.

It was supposed to be a great job offer: A full-time dream job and steady income. A part of me was thrilled. I had worked toward this since I started freelancing with this company and now they wanted me to join full-time. But at the same time, my lizard brain was going haywire. My palms were sweaty and my heart was suddenly beating fast. Was I about to lose everything again?

After being hit in the face with the harsh reality of my burned-out mental state and the challenges of the pandemic, I sold my business and restarted my working career as a remote coach on my own. I had slowly worked myself back into a better mental state, mostly thanks to my 3/2 workweek rhythm. I felt happy and productive, even if I wasn't earning my dream income yet. Everything was running smoothly and I was still recovering. Initially, I had planned to do more work for them in my dream role, but then I realized that came with a contract. And more responsibilities. Like weekly meetings.

Even though the contract did not list specific availability, it did list that I had to be responsive. It was planned as a remote job and I had a 6-hour time difference, but still, I was hesitant. Was this the end of my personal 3/2 workweek experiment? Would they notice it when I took 2 days off in the middle of the week? Would it be better to tell them ahead of time? Or would it be ok as long as my job performance was good? What if I still got my work done and I could provide a response within 24 hours—would they notice and fire me immediately for not upholding a standard workweek?

I was scared of taking the job and shifting out of the 3/2 workweek. Honestly, I was more afraid of what going back to my old ways would do to me, my productivity, and my health. I decided that I trusted the 3/2 method enough to let my productivity and results do the talking—I just had to learn to navigate the downsides (which you'll read more about in a later chapter). But before we get to that, we need to talk about the other benefits of fewer workdays.

In general, fewer working hours, the same productivity output, and less stressed employees all sound like big enough wins to convince us that this model is the way to go. But wait, as they often say in commercials, there's more!

Time to Reframe—Fewer Workdays and Company Costs

Flexible work times and fewer workdays reduce traffic volume and congestion during peak times by shifting the commutes of drivers into less congested periods. While we might think that increasing infrastructure alone could solve increased travel demands, a report on U.S. research explains that if you are able to expand the ability of people to travel, they are more likely to do it. This means that easier drives mean more trips in the car[47]. Any working model that isn't a Monday through Friday schedule with starting times around 8:00 to 9:00 am and finishing between 4:00 and 6:00 pm would help alleviate the burden of traffic.

The rush hour is costly in that time is lost because one is stuck in traffic (and time is money). By offering flexible starting times and workdays, congestion could be avoided and pressure taken off the infrastructure which, in most parts of the world, is dangerously close to reaching capacity.

As just one example, the researchers in the

Perpetual Guardian 4-day-week study estimated that flexible working models across industry in the city of Auckland would reduce the traffic congestion, saving the city $1.3 billion a year[48].

Solutions Offered by Flexible Working Arrangements

A flexible working arrangement can be anything from shift work to seasonal work. Then there are condensed workweeks or weekend work. But most of these are based on fitting the same 40 hours of a normal workweek into a different schedule. The 4-day workweek is the only known model that reduces hours while keeping the amount of pay the same. So, some of the well-researched advantages of the flexible work schedule might also be applicable to the 4-day workweek. The first advantage that pops out is cost reduction.

For example, if the parent of a sick child is able to take care of the child by working from home or working the needed hours later during the day, it is cheaper for the business than them taking a sick day.

Also, studies have shown that employees who have access to flexible working arrangements are happier employees[49]. Does this mean John Smith will just randomly not come in on a Thursday? Contrary to belief, flexible working arrangements don't foster more absenteeism, but quite the opposite: they reduce it. All policies and practices that enable employees to set their hours will help alleviate such work-life conflicts, which means worker well-being will be enhanced instead of diminished[Ibid].

But maybe the biggest impact of flexible working agreements is the opportunity flexible working arrangements have to build lasting relationships between employers and employees—managers and workers.

Can I ask you a question? How would you feel, if when you go to a restaurant, they would take your credit card details along with your order before they cooked or served your food? Even though it would be an easy thing for you to get up and leave without paying once you finish your food, there is inherent trust in you by the restaurant that you won't. That feels good, doesn't it? What if your server was panicking and asking you about the check every 5 minutes as you tried (and failed) to enjoy your meal? You're right. That wouldn't be a good experience.

Now, let's look at managers and employees through that same lens. If managers or companies don't trust their employees to get their work done in a timely manner by managing their own working time and commitments, what does that say about their relationship to that employee? What, in turn, would change if your boss was like: "Do whatever you want, as long as the work is done on time and reflects the good quality you know we expect. Does that work for you?" It is not like you are a freelancer doing your first (and possibly last) project with the company.

Companies that want to keep employees for 3, 5, and 10 years should have trust in the skills of those employees. In this better work world, the management doesn't feel the need to micromanage the time employees spend on their assigned tasks (or if they do, it's because they made the wrong hire). This practice would be the equivalent to, "We'll take your card after you've finished your meal, thanks." Shouldn't employees get at least the same amount of trust as we get at any restaurant we randomly visit for the first time?

The Perpetual Guardian experiment underlines just how significant this trust transfer can be: The feeling of empowerment went from 68% before the experiment, to 86% after it[50]. But even with all the positives we see in the 4-day workweek, there are still problems that need to be addressed.

The Shortcomings of the 4-Day Workweek

What the CEO behind the 4-day workweek experiment at Perpetual Guardian has been very vocal about is that the system does not "just work" if you go and turn a 2-day weekend into a 3-day weekend. This defeats the purpose of making the workweek more productive—all this does is make the workweek shorter. The trial of Perpetual Guardian showed that if the main goal (presented to the employees) is not to get the same amount of work done in less time, the 4-day workweek will fail[Ibid].

If none of your work strategies change, and employees essentially just finish the same week a day earlier on Thursday, the 4-day week is just that: A workweek that ends after 4 days. There needs to be a consistent and constant review of work practices to keep previous unproductive measures out of rotation. This has more to do with established habits than with the shorter weeks. The truth is, there needs to be some external factor that puts emphasis on productivity to make the shorter workweek just as productive as the 5/2 model.

When I was coaching clients in small group classes, do you know what made the difference between the people showing up once a week and those who showed up 4 times? It wasn't that the frequent visitors had more time than the others. All of their days had 24 hours. The difference was also unrelated to how much *free* time they had available, it was in how they *prioritized* it.

Yes, there were the 20-something students showing up 5 or 6 times a week—but there were also the single moms who worked full-time jobs making time to work out 5 hours a week (not including their commutes). The single biggest difference was never how much time they had, because we all have the same amount—we just choose to allot our time differently. The single moms had the willpower to put their exercise in one of their top 3 time slots. And that's the same willpower that's needed to make a 4-day workweek just as productive as a 5/2 workweek. Without that willpower, just shortening your workweek by 1 day won't focus your productivity for you.

We will see how the unique constellation of the 3/2 workweek emphasizes these changes even more, making it nearly impossible not to increase productivity while using this model.

The 4-Day Workweek Is an Improvement, But Is There a Better Way?

The 4-day week was a great success for everyone involved. It offered a traditional Pareto efficient change: a situation where no party was made worse off. In this case, no stakeholder was worse off. The employer still got the same amount of work from the employees. The workforce did not sacrifice any of their pay, but gained more free time. All the while, important performance indicators like employee stress levels decreased.

For society, such a model offers benefits on infrastructure costs—of course this flattens out if all companies were to switch to Monday through Thursday since morning and evening rush hours on

4 days would still remain the same. But what if there was a model based on the findings that could be even more flexible? One that takes into account the trends of remote work. Trust me when I say that there is additional potential here. And those pieces of potential are what we're going to cover next.

Key Takeaways

- Several companies have tested a 4-day workweek and found that it equals the 5/2 model in terms of output. The amazing benefit of this is that the workers get the same amount of pay.
- In an experimental 2-month period, Perpetual Guardian implemented a 4-day week, where productivity was at the same level as before, while both the commitment and empowerment of the staff increased.
- The country of Iceland has implemented the 4-day week in their administration (which, due to the size of the country amounts to 1% of total working population). Their productivity remains the same, but stress and burnout decreased with work-life balance improving.
- People naturally resist change because our brains are hardwired to keep us safe with "something that already works"—I also got the creeps when I was asked to go from part-time freelancer to full-time employee and almost stopped the 3/2 workweek.

But if your work and employer are truly about what you get done and not about representation hours, you'll be able to work something out (and I'll show you how in a later chapter).

- Fewer workdays save costs and decrease the general infrastructural load (and the dreadful hours of our lives we spend stuck in traffic.).
- The 4-day workweek has shortcomings: If you only shorten the week without adding any productivity goals, you will not succeed in changing habits, which can lead to not reaching the same productivity as the traditional 5/2 workweek.

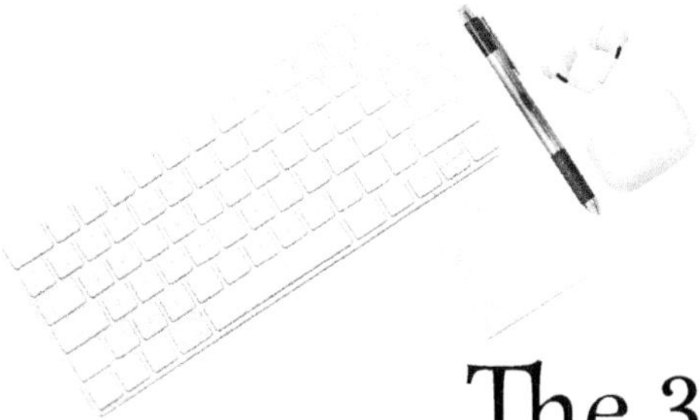

CHAPTER 7

The 3/2 Model Includes It All

Counting your days won't leave you with a life you look back on with a sense of accomplishment. Instead, you need to make each day count so that you can look back with gratitude and satisfaction.

When I work with fitness coaches or gym owners, we often talk about who their ideal clients are. An ideal client is someone they are not only extremely well equipped to help, but also someone I would say they "jive with." This is the kind of person they actually *enjoy* working with.

I'm sure if you're the kind of person who would read this book that you've heard about the 80/20 principle. It's usually used to describe the phenomenon that 20% of the customers bring in 80% of the sales. But there's a different way to interpret this principle when it comes to thinking about ideal clients.

Coaches and gym owners are entrepreneurs—and that means it is important to make sure that "riding the lion" is fun instead of terrifying for them. The best way to do this is to stay sharp and motivated. What does this have to do with ideal clients? In this scenario, the energy-sucking clients are too costly to keep. Let me explain.

Dealing with less-than-ideal clients can drain the life out of a business owner. So, once the incoming sales of the business covers the basic expenses, I no longer allow my clients to take non-ideal clients "just to fill their books." The energy drain just won't be worth the emotional toll in the long run.

When you work, you are just like an entrepreneur. Meetings aside, you are in charge of what you work on right now and the focus you dedicate to it. You can have days where you end up feeling accomplished and satisfied and you can have days that drain your hours without anything productive to show for them. And when it comes to motivation and focus, your "ideal clients" could be thought of as "ideal days," which will benefit you just as much.

Think about it: How do you feel when you leave work after a good, productive day? How do feel after an unproductive day? Which experience would you rather have? As a coach (both in fitness and of other business owners), I aim to stack small wins on top of each other while limiting setbacks for my clients. We know from motivation research that in the carrot-and-stick approach (where the carrot represents a reward and the stick represents punishment), the carrot is more successful[51].

So, if we have days where we know we are regularly underperforming in productivity, why bother at all? Why teach your working self that you can "get by" with a less-than-stellar day? These are both relevant questions, and as we explore the 3/2 workweek, we will explore the answers while simultaneously trashing traditional, end-of-workweek Fridays along with their diminished productivity.

If we want to find a model that strikes the delicate balance of increased productivity and employee well-being along with happiness, we must put measures in place that make use of the high productivity during the first days of the week.

As we saw earlier, Monday is traditionally the most productive day, with Tuesday closely trailing and Wednesday offering a slight falloff (but still within 95% of Monday). If most of our workdays held the same productivity of those first workdays, we would automatically increase performance without having to increase working time.

The 3 on, 2 off model makes use of that by having only 3 days in a row of work, followed by a break period. As we start work on Monday, we continue 3 days through Wednesday. Thursday and Friday would be off, like a 2-day weekend. Then the cycle starts anew, with 3 work days: Saturday through Monday.

Tuesday and Wednesday are off days, followed by another 3 days of work and so on. Please refer to the table below for details.

	MON	TUES	WED	THUR	FRI	SAT	SUN
1st week	work day 1	work day 2	work day 3	off	off	work day 1	work day 2
2nd week	work day 3	off	off	work day 1	work day 2	work day 3	off
3rd week	off	work day 1	work day 2	work day 3	off	off	work day 1
4th week	work day 2	work day 3	off	off	work day 1	work day 2	work day 3
5th week	off	off	work day 1	work day 2	work day 3	off	off
6th week Same as Week 1	work day 1	work day 2	work day 3	off	off	work day 1	work day 2

The 3/2 Model

This is a rotating 5-day schedule, with the 2 off days shifting through the weeks. That means that the 6th week looks like the 1st again. (In later chapters I will discuss different applications of this model that preserve a fixed weekend or more traditional Saturday/Sundays off while still benefiting from the 3/2 model's benefits.)

By increasing the frequency of the full 2-day weekend breaks, we also increase the theoretical amount of Mondays through Wednesdays in every month. This makes the fullest use of the high performing days, 1 through 3, back at work after your weekend. Essentially, instead of only having one Monday and Tuesday a week, we have 2 of each of them instead of the lesser productive Thursdays and Fridays. Furthermore, the reduction of the week to only 3 workdays keeps both productivity and motivation high. Remember how the short 4- or 3-day weeks feel before a long holiday weekend? The workweek usually seems like a breeze. During those weeks, you often get a large amount done in a short period of time.

This creates a schedule where every workday is your ideal workday. But let's be clear on one thing from the start: The goal is not to try and pack 4 or even 5 days into these 3 days by working longer hours each day. As we see from the 4-day workweek experiment, that won't be necessary to get to the same amount of productivity. Plus, it would defeat the purpose of leveraging the best productivity long-term.

When looking at the 3/2 model initially, it might seem like we're losing 2 workdays (going down from 5 to 3 workdays per workweek) but that isn't the case if you look at the total numbers for the month. When choosing a more comprehensive view, we see that not many working hours are lost compared to the 5/2, 40-hour week. Even if we just compare the naked total of days per month in each model—completely disregarding higher productivity altogether for the moment—there isn't a huge loss. Let's have a look at the exact breakdown.

Everyone knows they are less productive on Friday, and still, we drag ourselves into work just to chat up our colleagues and surf websites.

The Productivity Numbers of the 3/2 Method Compared to the 5/2 Workweek

An average, 30-day month in the traditional Monday to Friday workweek (the 5/2 method) has a total of 22 workdays. During the same period of time, the 3/2 workweek totals 18 workdays. This number of workdays matches the previously mentioned 4-day week model—so if we can get the same amount of work done in a 4-day workweek as we can in the traditional 5/2 model, the evidence points us to being able to do the same with the 3/2 workweek as well.

	3/2 Workweek	5/2 Workweek	4-Day Workweek
Work days	18	22	18
Days off	12	8	12
# of "Weekends"	6	4	4
# Mondays	6	4,3	4,3
# Tuesdays	6	4,3	4,3
# Wednesdays	6	4,3	4,3

Monthly Totals of Varying Workweek Methods

But how does this shake out if we compare the productivity of the days worked in the different models?

Based on the productivity numbers of Redbooth[52], starting with the most productive day (Monday) as being worth 100 points, we can calculate the relative productivity of the other days. In this fashion, Tuesday is 99 points, and Wednesday 95 points, while Thursday and Friday drop to 91 points and 82 points respectively. So, in the 5/2 model the 4 additional days every month are days that average a productivity of 86.5%. In the 3/2 model, the Monday through Wednesday work days come in at an average of 98%.

The "lost" days of the month in the 3/2 model are the days where it is proven that workers have the lowest productivity anyway. So, the question becomes: Would you rather keep the 4 additional days at 86.5% productivity or trade them for 6 more Mondays, Tuesdays, or Wednesdays with their 98% productivity?

MONDAY	TUESDAY	WEDNESDAY	THURSDAY	FRIDAY
100	0.99	0.95	0.91	0.82

*Average productivity based on Monday = 100	AVERAGE MON-WED	AVERAGE THU-FRI
	100	86.5

Average Productivity Throughout Week by Workday

This does not include any additional productivity that shorter weeks would offer. Looking at the experience of the 4-day workweek established by Perpetual Guardian, where the amount of work of 5 days was successfully completed in 4 days, it is highly likely that during the 3 days of the 3/2 workweek, an even higher productivity in fewer hours is likely. This means it would end with at least the same total output as the 4-day model.

Higher productivity is a benefit for employee and employer alike. Let's remember one thing: We are not working days for the sake of logging hours behind a desk. Our main interest is the output that the workdays create. Taking the mathematical approach further, a comparison of the calculated productivity shows that the 3/2 model has a higher total productivity rate than the 4-day workweek, which we know from application can offer at least the same productivity as the 5-day week.

In a practical setting we can therefore expect the 3/2 model to outperform the 4-day workweek in terms of productivity (and thereby also the 5/2 as the practical application has shown). But the 3/2 method comes with an additional benefit to the 4-day workweek: It has 6 weekends instead of 4.

Enjoying 6 Weekends a Month Instead of 4

	3/2 Workweek	5/2 Workweek	4-Day Workweek
Work days	18	22	18
Productive day score (1-100)	98%	93%	96%
Days off	12	8	12
# of "Weekends"	6	4	4

Productive Days in Varying Models

The 4-day workweek and the 3/2 model both have more free days than the traditional 5/2 workweek. With 12 days off instead of 8, both alternative models offer time off at a whopping increase of 33% (4 days), so employees have a significant amount of extra free time to spend as they please.

The substantial difference between the 4-day workweek and the 3/2 method is how those free days are spread out. In the 4-day workweek, we get longer weekends, whereas the 3/2 workweek adds 2 full weekends over the course of the month. This also means that the working period is no longer than 3 days before the employee gets another break. This does bounds for the happiness of employees while giving them more time to recharge.

Given that you would have the same amount (12 days) off in the 4-day work model as well, the big advantage is that the 3/2 method has the off days spread out more often, making the working stretches shorter. But this is only valuable if you make sure to take advantage of what your free days have to offer. So, let's discuss that next.

The Benefits of Shutting Off Through Weekends

How you spend your weekends *does* matter. The ability to shut off and recover during the weekend has been proven to have an effect on weekly task performance, personal initiative, organizational behavior and perceived low efforts[53]. In other words: If you are able to shut off, your next week will be more productive.

More weekends in this equation mean more opportunities to shut off. More shutting off equals more time to recharge and come back with extra energy to be productive. So, on the other side, if we fall into the trap of taking some work home or logging into our computers to complete tasks during our weekends, we are taking away from the next week's productivity. There is simply no truth to the idea that "more is more." More becomes less after 30 to 35 hours. Period.

Adding More Life to the Work-Life Balance

Now you know that the 3/2 workweek significantly increases the number of weekends in a month (adding

33% of free time). Additionally, the stretch in between 2 weekends is only 3 days, instead of the regular 5. This adds more "life" to the "work-life balance." And it's not only Generation Z that values more days off over financial benefits[54]—if we could get the same done in less time, be paid the same amount, and have more free time, who wouldn't want that? It sounds almost too good to be true.

While not all of those days off fall on traditional weekends, this can actually be a great advantage: Have you ever tried to make it to a government appointment or meeting with your bank when their operating hours are 9:00 am to 4:00 pm, Monday through Friday? Or get an appointment with your doctor? Usually, it's a tightrope walk between getting an appointment soon enough and not missing too many hours of work (or spending your last sick day on a 15-minute appointment).

If you live in a suburban area or work long hours, you might even struggle to get groceries once in a while. The stress of having to juggle such errands with a 5/2 workweek can be enormous. The middle-of-the-week days off solve this problem. It's also great to beat the crowds when you have errands to run or want to enjoy free-time activities.

What about tangible results? The employees in the 4-day week trial reported that they *particularly* enjoyed the non-weekend off day. Having an extra day off to themselves with no spouse around, no work, or no children underfoot allowed them to catch up on things or get some "me time" that was much needed[55]. But what about the flip side of the 3/2 workweek? What happens when one of your work days lands on a Saturday or Sunday? Do those days feel sad and like they've been wasted? Let's find out.

The Benefits of Having Workdays on Saturday and Sunday

Working on a Saturday or Sunday is something that might seem strange at first, but after you've tried it, you will see how productive it can be. In fact, as I talked about this model and book with friends, the most common reaction of employees without kids was "That would be great, I could get so much done on a Sunday when I don't have customer calls or need to meet with colleagues." This environment offers the benefit that efficiency nerds discovered for themselves a long time ago: There is unique power in blocks of time that are single-task designated because of fewer interruptions.

This ultra-focused work has been hailed as the superpower of the 21st century. In his book *Deep Work*, Cal Newport says that being able to perform what he calls "deep work" is becoming more and more rare as it is also more actively sought because of its value to our economy. He also says that the biggest consequence of this is that those who can manage deep work and make it part of who they are will be able to live and work in a way that allows them to thrive[56].

The developments of the past 30 years, including the uptick of open office spaces for rent combined with bringing instant messaging systems into the work environment over the last 5 to 10 years, have created major speed bumps to productivity. Focus—made possible by uninterrupted time—is becoming rare. Often, it is not easy to escape these unending distractions in traditional work environments. Deep work is much more likely in a remote or 3/2 model work setting.

So, while the deepest wish of the employer is to have happy and productive employees, all the tools they have introduced into the work environment have fostered the complete opposite result. Without turning everything topsy-turvy, the 3/2 workweek is the solution employees need to thrive in the modern workforce—ensuring the personal happiness of workers, which in turn delivers an above average productivity.

Key Takeaways

- The 3/2 model and the 4-day workweek have the exact same number of workdays over a month. Since the 4-day workweek has been proven to equal the 5/2 model in terms of work getting accomplished (productivity), the same will be true for the 3/2 method.
- The biggest difference between the 4-day workweek and the 3/2 model is that there are more weekends per month: 6 instead of 4. This means breaks are more frequent.
- Working Saturdays and Sundays and, in turn, having days off in the middle of the week creates several advantages. First, the quiet non-customer-facing weekends come with fewer interruptions. Second, the middle-of-the-week days off are great for getting things like appointments in, which reduces stress while increasing the life part of one's work-life balance.

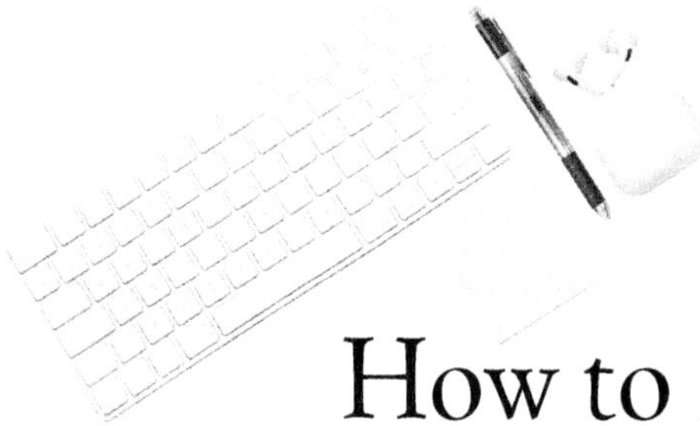

CHAPTER 8

How to Switch to a 3 On, 2 Off Workweek

Instead of trying to do more, what if we did less work, but got better results?

So, you decided to go ahead and switch to the 3/2 model, huh? Great! But does this mean that if you set a starting date (next Monday!) you're ready to go? Well, you will be after you read this chapter, which dives into how to take the first step and navigate any obstacles that might appear along the way.

Since some challenges are general and others are specific to your work or employment structure, I will go through the different obstacles you might face specifically as an employee, boss, or parent toward the end of this chapter. Right now, let's address the more general issues. First, I want to start with the elephant in the room: How the hell are you going to fit all your work into just 3 days?

I'll answer that question in a minute, but before we get to that, can I tell you a story? I was sweating, but not from heat or exercise. Instead, I was dripping with sweat caused by sheer panic. We only had 1 workday left and we had nothing. No slides, no samples, no visuals, no marketing strategy, or overview of the marketing budget—and we were meeting the potential buyer the next day!

I was working in the Sales and Key Account Management department for a chocolate manufacturer. We always pre-sold seasonal items to our largest buyer first—and that was the meeting looming over our heads, less than 24 hours away. This was a make-it-or-break-it presentation: Whatever they bought would be feasible and profitable for our company to produce and distribute to smaller buyers as well.

If you don't remember the last time you gained a few pounds from holiday chocolate: 30% of the chocolate industry's sales revenue is made during the Easter and Christmas holiday seasons. It was on us, the Sales team, to present the new products, have the buyer taste them, paint them a magnificent picture of a strategy to help them market the items, and then get them to sign the dotted line for as many chocolate bunnies as possible. If they didn't like our presentation, the yearly sales targets and whole company were in trouble.

The problem with this being the first buyer was that our R&D, production, packaging design, and marketing departments had to prepare everything in time for us to put together a stellar presentation—and they were usually and collectively a bit late. But this year it they seemed too late: At 4:00 pm the day before the presentation we still had no information whatsoever. Sales people often get a bad rap for selling clients things by concocting facts out of thin air, but I didn't feel like creating made-up facts matched my personal skill set. I've never been the kind of salesperson who could sell ice blocks to a penguin (even though my sales attire—a black suit with white shirt—has made me look a bit like a penguin in the past).

As this was ultimately one of the single most important sales pitches for the entire company, we'd usually start the preparation weeks before. This time it was 5:00 pm when we got the information along with the graphics. So, we did the only thing we could: We put our heads down. In one gigantic feat, working until midnight, we threw the presentation together (the timing had nothing to do with Cinderella getting home, but instead hinged on the last train connection).

We familiarized ourselves with and bolstered the selling points. We printed and cut out mock-ups of packaging we didn't have yet. We prepped the samples that we got through a same-day-express service and put them on platters. And we sweated, a lot.

In the end, we managed to pull off the impossible: Everything was ready the next morning to present to the customer. What I remember feeling during the presentation was extra nervous energy. I was just waiting to be unmasked as a crooked salesperson. But thankfully, for both me and my armpits, we made the sale.

I remember on the way back to the car, a big pat on the back from my boss who said, "We pulled it off! Thank you for going the extra mile. Let this be a lesson to you that impossible things can be done in an impossible timeline when you set your mind to it. Not that we'll ever be doing that again! From now on, we'll make sure to get our information sooner. But now we know what we are capable of, if we have to do something similar again."

He had summed up what I had felt. If given the choice, we would've spent weeks preparing for the meeting. Yet, the outcome would not have been any better. We wouldn't have sold more bunnies. We got the job done within a *ridiculous* timeline. Though not per choice, I had discovered a newfound tool that allowed me to be extremely productive. I learned that when you have limited time, it can heighten your focus.

I'm sure you have experienced similar situations to this—like when you have one day until you leave on vacation and you know you have to get everything on your to-do list done. Isn't it magic how suddenly you accomplish 3 or 4 times as many tasks as usual? This is one big advantage you'll harness consistently with the 3/2 workweek if you do it right.

Embracing the New Schedule: Batching and Pruning Your Calendar

At this point in your workweek assessment journey, it is important to keep an open mind and embrace your new schedule with all the freedom and productivity it will bring. You will quickly learn that implementing a 3/2 workweek automatically creates 2 essential elements to both happiness and productivity: batching and pruning.

The first one we need to go through is batching. Batching is a word that originates from computer programming. To save memory and power, similar computer tasks get batched to run together at a certain time instead of being spread throughout the day. If you collect your invoices in a pile to pay them once a week, you are batching your bill payments, only requiring you to log into your bank account once and knock out multiple invoices at once, which saves you time.

The second term and method—pruning—has to do with creating the biggest pumpkin possible. By cutting weaker branches and smaller flowers off plants, also known as pruning, farmers have been making it possible to grow pumpkins the size of a compact car (the heaviest ever pumpkin weighed in at 2,700 pounds or 1.2 tons[57]!). Pruning concentrates the plant's energy (provided by water and nutrients) on fewer, high potential branches. Instead of creating a vast net of flowers and fruits, the plant is able to focus all its resources on growing one (hopefully gigantic) pumpkin.

What if we did the same with our sparse resources to better focus our attention on one thing at a time instead of trying to multitask ourselves to exhaustion? Imagine what work could be like if any day was like your last day before vacation. The challenge is, how do we impose the associated pressure of having to focus and finish tasks quickly during a regular week? Unfortunately, it is very hard to do this artificially. Pretending you have a vacation coming up won't cut it. That's why looming external deadlines have always worked. That's how our team pulled off our giant sales presentation in just a couple of hours. In the 3/2 method, there is an equally compelling deadline looming.

"I've only got 2 days," is a real deadline: It's exactly the thing that makes you uncomfortable enough to stop looking for excuses to use that justify your midday social media break. In fact, pruning is one of your most important productivity tools. So let's look at both batching and pruning more closely.

In the 3/2 model, batching happens as you plan tasks and meetings that are client-facing or include colleagues that use a 5/2 workweek, solely around your 3 or 4 midweek workdays. Since you can only align with them during certain times based on both of your schedules, you will find yourself much more efficient when it comes to allotting your Monday to Friday days to meetings.

This in turn creates big blocks of undisturbed working time on your weekend workdays. You might even find that clients (or co-workers) enjoy your new Saturday availability if you offer it to them. Simply by asking yourself what you need to fit into each kind of day, you will find yourself pruning your tasks and meetings down to the essentials and creating blocks of focused working time.

Let me emphasize this again: Big changes are not accomplished by merely adjusting old, familiar approaches. The 3/2 method will be a big change. And the first step is to let go of what you think your work schedule needs to be.

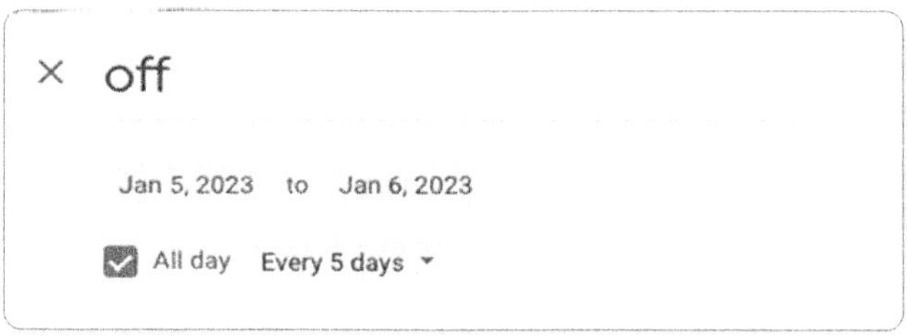

It's Okay to Set Your Schedule to "Off"
No Matter What Day of the Week it Is

The first step you need to take is to choose to let go of any anxiety connected to taking a midweek day off. Start out by setting up whatever calendar you use to reflect your new workday and off-day schedule. I do recommend a digital calendar because you can easily implement the 3/2 rotation and later link scheduling tools directly into your availability.

In your digital calendar of choice, block your 4th and 5th day as busy and choose a repeat set to "every 5 days." Your calendar will automatically be populated with your off days and your scheduling availability will be blocked for any days off. Congrats, that wasn't too hard, was it?

As you start out your new 3/2 workweek, you will also plan for your new "mini week" of 3 workdays at a time instead of 5. That means assigning the tasks in the order they need to be done within those 3 days. What is vital during these 3 days and what can wait until your next mini week? Look ahead to when your next 3-day workweek will be and think about what task and deadlines fall within those days. This will help you prune so you can decide what makes the list and what gets pushed to the next work block.

Next, embrace the advantages of a classic 5/2 workweek, where Friday means close of business. Each month you will have workdays on Saturday and/or Sunday! If you need to, specify with colleagues and clients which ones need to have your work by Monday morning. This is just one way your schedule will be more flexible than others' and you can use this to your benefit.

On Saturdays and Sundays, it is ideal to make your work batch focused. For example, you could prioritize administrative work that does not require any customer or colleague feedback. These will also be the days where you can get the most creative or high-focus work done. There is one thing you should think about between Monday and Friday no matter what your 3/2 schedule looks like, so let's talk about that next.

Learn to Be "Off" During the Week, But Keep a 24-Hour Response Time

After you get over the shock of not always having regular Saturday/Sunday weekends, there's another big obstacle to tackle next: going MIA for 2 days in the middle of the week. This was my biggest fear when I was asked to go from a freelancer to a full-time employee. What if I missed an important thing? What if my employer got mad? Should I be open and disclose my 3/2 workweek schedule to them, or should I fly under the radar and just fix things that happened as they popped up?

Being able to put an "Out of Office" responder in, or being open with your boss, colleagues, or clients about your 3/2 work schedule and all its benefits will naturally make it the easiest for you to keep your off days completely off, even during the week. But maybe you aren't currently in a place where you feel confident doing this just yet. In that situation, how do you keep up with necessary response times even when you have your 2 free days in the middle of the standard workweek?

Generally, a 24-hour response time is the accepted worldwide norm, so let's start there. To truly keep a

24-hour response time, all you need to do is log into your emails or messages exactly once per day on your off days. For example, if you last checked your inbox at 4:00 pm the day before your midweek weekend, you need to check them again at or shortly before 4:00 pm on your first day off. Then check them at the same time on your second day off.

But beware: This is not about going through everything in your inbox and processing every single new email—this is just checking for urgent and important pieces of correspondence and answering them.

Before you start your first 3/2 workweek, make a list what type of emails or actions really require a 24-hour response time during your Monday through Friday "off days." Be honest about what is really important, which is different from what is expected. Chances are you work in a job where nobody will die if they don't get a response from you within 24 hours. There won't be any train wrecks just because you aren't available. My list looks like this:

- New client inquiries
- Client medical emergencies

That's it. My complete list.

After you have defined which items warrant a response within 24 hours, you will know what to scan your inbox for. This designated scan is the sole purpose of this short amount of time you look into your inbox. Done correctly and focused in such a way, it should take no longer than 15 to 20 minutes to scan and respond to the types of messages on your list that warrant an immediate reply.

Learn to keep it at that. If you want to get really fancy, you can use a virtual assistant or set up a filter to forward only those types of messages to you or your voicemail. This can help if you find it difficult to resist the temptation of going down the rabbit hole, reading through emails that aren't on your list, or if you can't compartmentalize your thoughts enough to avoid worrying about those unread emails for the rest of your off day.

The more you implement this system, the more you will learn that very few things actually require you to be available within 24 or even 2 hours (I heard you nervous bunch in the back shouting "What if I need to respond even sooner than within 24 hours?"). If you find this difficult, or that the 24-hour rule is insufficient, have a thorough look at your work environment.

The company I work for very rarely has 24-hour deadlines on any responses. Oftentimes, if a work emergency presents itself via email, it is because someone else has forgotten something. If others are commonly sending you demanding emails because they dropped the ball when they were supposed to take care of a task, this is hard to deal with on your end (since it's their responsibility). So, the more urgent requests there are, the more it points to a disorganized or mismanaged project, or a faulty company culture. If that is your situation, it is probably time to rethink your job.

While we can all forget tasks sometimes—working in an environment where everything seems to be urgent all the time will wear you out no matter what work schedule you choose. Sometimes, this means the best choice you can make is to set healthy boundaries by looking for a new job where every message isn't marked as urgent. I know this sounds scary. But there is a Native American saying that goes: "If you realize you are riding a dead horse, get off."

Pro Tip: Use Automatic Responders

If you can't stick to the system of just checking for and responding to the kind of messages and emails you put on your list of critical items, it's time to implement the trusted vacation responder. You can have your responder set to 2 days of being absent, or try an always-active responder with a hint that you only check mails at a certain time of the day. I have seen this implemented in traditional 5/2 workplaces in order to get more uninterrupted working blocks and to manage (and curate) expectations. If you find yourself (or colleagues) struggling with taking longer time off from emails, you should try an email like the one in the following example:

Subject: Limited Email Responses

"Thank you for your email. I only check my email once a day at (INSERT YOUR TIME). I will get back to you within that time frame. If you believe your enquiry is an urgent matter, please message me at: .... This is my private number—the same one my mom uses to call me. So please use it with care."

I was first introduced to this method of framing by an author who claimed he had never had anyone misuse his number or disregard his personal down time after he had framed his response this way. By handing the responsibility of recognizing the level of urgency to the enquirer, you are also giving them trust.

They will have to consciously ask themselves if their question warrants such time-sensitivity. And 99.9% of them will come to the correct answer. The few that don't will communicate their clear misalignment with your values and goals through this choice. And this is the kind of information you like to know about a client sooner rather than later. And now that we have emails covered, let's turn to the next item that probably popped into your head: What about meetings?

Navigating Weekly Meetings

What do you do about weekly recurring meetings? First things first: Start pruning! I encourage you to challenge the current narrative and dig deep to determine which meetings are really necessary on a weekly, 7-day rotational basis. Here is what I see happen on the regular: someone is missing from the meeting, the project is waiting for the client's feedback, or there is nothing new to report. One or all 3 circumstances combined often render a weekly meeting completely pointless.

But since the meeting time is set and blocked, you find other things to talk about. What was supposed to be a productive meeting turns into a chat about Janet's baked goods that are waiting in the break room—all because you have blocked the hour anyway. So instead of having fixed weekly and biweekly meetings you don't use to the full extent, have them on a case-by-case basis. The other option is to set the new meeting time at every end of the session using the natural pattern within the 3/2 workweek—this way you can work around your available workdays. In the 3/2 workweek, a pattern for rotation that always works is biweekly, biweekly, weekly repeat. So, in a 5-week period you'd have 3 meetings, and then repeat this rhythm over again.

At first, it might seem complicated if you need to align meetings with regular 5/2 method co-workers on the fewer days you are available Monday through Friday. But this also offers a great opportunity to tighten up your meeting days and productive workdays.

This distinction between actual working time

and meeting time is not new. Productivity books and employees have been aware of this issue for ages. In fact, I believe this is the sole reason for the uptick of the 4:00 am wake up-and-work trend—as well as the urge to stay in for long evenings (after one's work-interrupting colleagues have gone home).

If we know about this problem, why haven't we found a sustainable solution yet? Because the pressure to say "No!" and remove yourself from these situations hasn't been high enough, yet. This is a great advantage of the 3/2 workweek. The way the workdays fall and are more concentrated, which means you must prune. With that in mind, my advice to you would be: Do not let up on this point just because it seems like a big ask. Understand that humans are creatures of habit and acknowledge that the 7-day rhythm rules the world. And in many cases, this is why weekly meetings were set up, not because they are actually necessary.

Move as many updates as you can to email form. Scratch general, weekly project-update type meetings altogether. Instead, ask the participant or participants to update you when they have made substantial progress. Then you can get a meeting on the calendar if they really need it.

One easy option for weekly meetings where the 3/2 method and the 5/2 workweek can match up is to agree on 2 meeting possibilities that are exactly 4 days apart: Monday or Thursday, Tuesday or Friday. You will always be able to make either one or the other.

As a rule of thumb, I recommend that you clear even your midweek off days to be completely off. But if weekly meetings stand in the way, here are some rules that allow you to at least keep most of those off days work free. You should only allow meetings to be scheduled during off days if the 2 following conditions are met.

- You are meeting with a hierarchical superior and/or 2 or more people.
- The meeting can be virtual and allows you to "dial in" from anywhere you are.
- Your total meeting time on the off day does not exceed 1 hour.

But remember, meetings on off days are to be an exception. All other meetings should be rescheduled or postponed. If possible, you could also excuse yourself from the meeting or ask a colleague to take notes you can use to catch up later.

I can't stress this enough: Don't be afraid to miss meetings! Meetings are rarely a productive use of your time. This is even more true when meetings include 4 or more people. Remind yourself that people miss meetings all the time due to sickness, travel, or holidays. If there are no clear meeting notes, summaries, follow-up emails, or recordings provided, make sure to get the notes you might need from a colleague. With the 3/2 schedule strictly enforced, you would only miss 2 out of 5 meetings if they are weekly and you don't have an option to call in. That is totally manageable.

But better efficiency doesn't stop at canceling meetings you can avoid. You can also be more efficient in meetings that can't be skipped. Let's talk about how.

An Essential Meeting—A Cheat Sheet (You're Welcome)

How to Streamline Meetings

Next to cutting down the non-essential meetings, the next important skill to learn is how to streamline meetings that make the cut. Get as many meetings into a virtual format as possible—they offer you more flexibility to navigate potential off days. (Of remote workers surveyed, 70% agree that virtual meetings are less stressful[58].) This option not only allows you to take meetings from anywhere, but also saves time it would normally take you to get to and from the meeting place (or the office). Make sure to get a fail-safe calendar with reminders and set them the necessary 5, 10, or 15 minutes in advance so you can get ready. If necessary, set 2 or 3 alarms, the first at a prep time, the second at a "get there" or "log in" time and the last one at the start time.

If you are organizing or co-organizing meetings, limit durations to a total of 30 minutes. The 4-day week trial at Perpetual Guardian found that by reducing meetings from 60 to 30 minutes, the meetings were run more efficiently and were more focused, saving both time and energy[59].

Another way to streamline is to use online scheduling tools linked to your calendar to decrease time spent searching for available meeting times with your colleagues. Don't underestimate this: The tail end of a meeting can be up to 10 minutes of exchanging availabilities.

"Does Tuesday work for you?"

"Generally, yes, but sorry, that particular Tuesday I have an out of town appointment. How would Friday afternoon work for you?"

"So sorry, Friday afternoons are usually busy, but I can fit 30 minutes in before 11."

If you have 1:1 meetings, use these tools for your meeting counterpart to schedule the next meeting rather than spending a substantial time of the meeting each flipping through calendars trying to find a time to align.

The virtual format also stops several conjunct discussions from going on at once, helping everyone to focus on one thread of discussion and only speak up if they have something important to say. This naturally makes meetings more efficient.

Resist the Urge to Make Workdays Longer

Like the employees who went through the 4-day week trial, you might be tempted to work longer days as you switch into the 3/2 model just to "compensate for what you feel is lost time." I want to stress again, that this would defeat the main point. Establishing systems to improve your state of mind will make you more productive. Adding hours won't increase productivity.

I generally do not recommend adding hours, especially at the start of your transition to the 3/2 model. With that being said, if you really stick to your 2 off days, you might be able to better recover from longer days (over 8 hours worked) than you would in a 5/2 model. But don't abuse this so you can avoid important pruning and batching decisions—these are just as essential to getting big benefits out of this system as trying to keep the off days off. Make it a priority for you to end your workdays on time. Also, ending at a decent hour will be one of the biggest contributors to maintaining your social life even if your friends work Monday through Friday.

But will this system really succeed if you don't work longer? Yes, as long as you don't allow yourself an easy cop-out. Think of my Easter bunny sales presentation or your last 2 days before you head out of the office for a holiday. Although your to-do list is huge, you succeed in getting everything done before leaving on vacation. The reason for this is that instead of approaching your work with the mindset "I have the next 2 weeks with 8 hours every day to get this done"—you know you only have 2 days left to get everything turned in (so you can fly out for your well-deserved beach trip).

Your departure time is set in stone—just like my meeting with the buyer was. That means you have a fixed amount of time in which you should and try to get the most done. In economics, the latter is known as getting the maximum return for a fixed amount of investment (in this example time is fixed).

This phenomenon is not new: Parkinson's law states that the work will expand to fill the time we allot it to[60]. That means if you give yourself the possibility to work for 12 hours instead of 8, your work tasks will tend to take more time than they would if you were set on hitting a non-negotiable 8 hours.

Have you ever had a day when you didn't have many meetings and your to-do list was shorter? You know, one of those days where you actually think "I'll get done with my stuff easily today!" I'd be willing to bet a lunch with you (on me) that you were not as efficient as you would have been on a day with a time-crunch. Or remember getting an assignment with a due date 6 months away? If you even touched the project, you probably did so in an unproductive way.

Now we know that tight deadlines help motivate us (even the ones we make ourselves). But what happens when we apply those same ideas to micro tasks like messaging the boss back on a communication app? Let's find out.

How to Handle Messengers like Slack, Teams, etc.

Recently, the popularity of instant messaging systems has been on the rise. You know, Slack, Teams, or whatever else they're called. Hailed as the one thing that will save us from receiving too many email messages every day or having to physically be in the same place as our teammates, messaging software has become a Hydra-type beast: Cut off one head and it grows two more.

You respond to a question, only to receive a follow-up 1 minute later. What might seem to fall into the "under 2 minutes, respond immediately" category can end up taking 15 minutes or more. First, you spend 5 minutes each to disentangle yourself from the train of thought the message interrupted. Then it takes another 5+ minutes to respond and for the subsequent back-and-forth that inevitably happens.

The creators of Basecamp, one of the first companies to put remote working into practice before it became a necessity (and coincidentally creators of online collaboration and client management software) have come up with some helpful guidelines on how to use these instant messengers and leverage their good, without falling prey to the bad and the ugly.

Establish planned chatting hours and allow every employee to set their own times to correspond with their least productive work times. These are to be set as hours where they are known to be available for instant messaging. For example, Jon's times are Tuesday and Thursday, 1:00 to 3:00 pm. If you have a question, it needs to wait until then—if it's urgent (oh what a surprise) you should try to problem solve on your own to figure out a way forward without having to interrupt Jon.

This might seem to be the complete opposite approach that many companies take. They often emphasize that employees should "inform us when you are *not* reachable for immediate responses" or they curate everyone's "Out of Office" calendars. But here is the conundrum with expecting every employee to *always* be available to respond within minutes during their working hours (and sometimes way beyond finishing time): It costs the most skilled and well-paid workers their most valuable working time.

If Jon is the one who is the expert on customer relationship software, he is not only the one who can solve those problems the more quickly, he is the one who will get interrupted the most, by all the other 1-100 employees who have any questions about the software.

For the newbie, Mary, who has not made it to page

30 of the manual yet, this is great. "I'll just message Jon and have the answer within seconds." For Jon, this means 1-100 interruptions each every 5 to 15 minutes, costing him (and the company) valuable uninterrupted working time in his expert field.

Let's imagine instant messaging was not available or not framed as an instant-reply service: Mary would either work on something else until she could ask the question (on Tuesday or Thursday) or keep reading the manual until she figured it out herself. Both these situations would spare Jon's valuable time while still offering a productive solution.

Here is what companies and bosses need to ask themselves: Do they want work to get done (and get out of the employee's way to do that work uninterrupted) or do they want to make everyone keep one eye on their messaging software, never fully enabling them to concentrate on the task at hand? And is it worth the resulting mediocre work to have employees ready to respond any minute? They can't have both quality work and constantly distracted workers. They need to decide what they are going to prioritize.

And now that we've talked quite a bit about the work side of 3 on, 2 off, let's get to the good part. It's finally time to talk about the 2 days off.

Spending Quality Time With Friends

We've covered the "how to" of the 3/2 model for work, now let's get into the flip side. You might think that the 3/2 model will make it difficult to find quality time with friends. In the beginning, so did I! But what I have found during these 2 years is that most social interactions happen in the evenings, so it becomes much more important to end your workday at a decent time than to make sure you have the same days off.

The single biggest thing getting in the way of quality time with friends and family is not ending your days on time (you know, aside from getting up and starting at ungodly hours, which—let's be honest—only very few actually *want* to do if given the choice). The best option for true productivity, which will get you out of work before you're too exhausted to eat or sleep, comes from the batching and pruning that happens with the 3/2 workweek.

To reiterate, if you are worried the 3/2 model might interfere with your free time with your friends and family, do everything you can to agree on a non-negotiable workday end time with yourself and stick to it. Also, you will still have days off that fall on regular weekends—and you'll know well in advance when those will happen. This knowledge encourages you to be purposeful by planning weekend things like a 2-day hiking trip with your 5/2 workweek friends well in advance. The truth is, you will always know months in advance when you will have weekends off.

If you'd rather you all went together to an almost deserted beach on a Tuesday or Wednesday, make sure to get your friends using the 3/2 workweek as well. By the way, we do offer bundle book prices if you go to 3on2off.com/book 😉.

Key Takeaways

- I once had to prep a very important sales presentation in 7 hours the day before the meeting (instead of 3 weeks we usually got to plan). But we made it work and sold all the Easter bunnies.
- The 3/2 method depends first on batching: planning similar tasks, or meetings together in blocks of time or on specific days so that you can create other big uninterrupted work time blocks.
- The 3/2 method also depends on pruning: concentrating on the few, important tasks (and meetings) and cutting away everything else.
- The heaviest pumpkin to ever grow (through pruning) weighs 1.5 tons.
- Your work will take the time you allot for it. This is called Parkinson's law. This is the reason you should have a non-negotiable end time and resist the urge to work longer. (A set end time is also the best way to still spend quality time with friends and family that follow the 5/2 workweek.)
- Avoid scheduling and attending weekly meetings—most of them are not necessary.

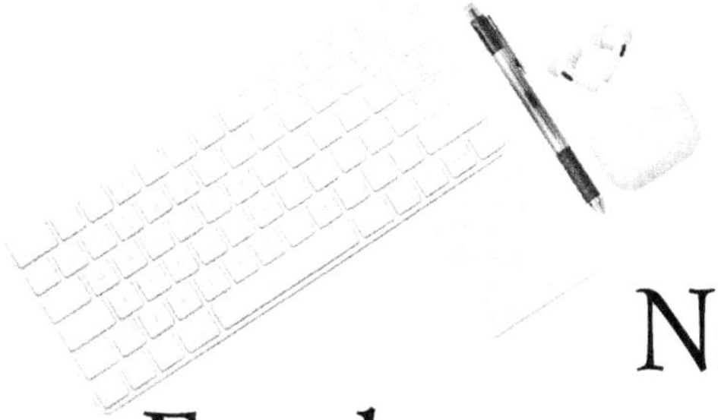

CHAPTER 9

Navigating Employment-Related Obstacles

You can't assume anyone else will provide you with a healthy work-life balance—especially not your boss. You have to create it for yourself.

Even though we are no longer stuck in Fordesque years of factory-bound work, the general feeling that employees need to be present on certain days and during core hours is still widely prevalent—especially if you have a "helicopter boss" that likes to hover over every move you make.

Let's get one thing out of the way: I grant you permission to work for outcomes instead of logging hours for the sake of being present. If you were looking for that permission, there you go. Stop worrying about the hours you put in. Instead, worry about the outcome and your effectiveness. You are no longer an

8-year-old who is required to follow the class schedule and only take breaks at exact times. And you will not get called out or punished if you adapt a schedule that makes you happier and maximizes your productivity in the long run. (Or if you do get detention, you should think about switching schools as soon as possible!)

As long as it is Pareto-efficient—meaning no party is worse off[61]—why should anyone be upset? And if you are worried that somebody might notice, here is your way out: In her article "Why Some Men Pretend to Work 80-Hour Weeks," Erin Reid explains research revealed that managers can't tell the difference between who is actually working 80 hours and who is just pretending to[62]. And that leads us right into our next point, because achieving a healthy work-life balance isn't about appearances.

Work-Life Balance is Often Not Balanced at All

Let's talk about work-life balance. Balance is about give-and-take. Both sides of the scale should have equal weights. The problem is, usually, that work tends to put its big fat finger on the scale. In response, our lives (like time with our spouse or free time with our friends or enjoying our hobbies), fly off one side and onto the floor in response to the tipping scale.

In this manner, work just keeps on taking.

And whenever you have something like a dentist appointment, it feels like a gigantic weight you have to counterweigh immediately with some late-hour or weekend work to prevent things from tipping further off balance. We have a hard time giving back on the life side what we gave away to work. As a rule: If work is allowed to sneak in after 5:00 pm on the regular, private things should have the same allowance so that we can sometimes shorten a workday to 3:00 or 4:00 pm!

Or as a past manager of mine once shared with me, "Life is a juggling act. You are always trying to keep more balls up in the air than you have hands. But the thing about these balls is, that the work-related balls are made of rubber. If you happen to drop one now and then, you just pick them up again and continue your juggling as if nothing happened. No permanent damage is done. But the private ones, your mental and physical health—those are made of glass. And there will be lasting consequences when you drop one."

If your week's work is done at 2:00 pm on Friday, it is no use to anyone if you just sit there until you feel it is "a socially acceptable time to leave the office" or log off. It's better to take some much needed recovery time. Plus, you sitting there waiting is not getting anything done for your boss.

To make things simpler, think about your options this way: You basically have 3 possibilities.

3 Possibilities for Employment-Based Obstacles to the 3/2 Method

1) Get official permission by your employer or direct supervisor to go all in on this proven method.
2) Implement it without asking, but alter the method in a way that it won't be recognized (and in turn possibly lessen your potential and the effectiveness of these methods)
or
3) Do it full scale, no permission, no regrets. Maybe disclose what you're doing later when you've already established a track record for getting stellar work done on time. (And leave them asking what your tricks are because they want to adapt your system for everyone so that they have more rock stars just like you).

Here is where I say that whatever you read in this book, what action you take is completely your choice. I take no responsibility for anything that happens. (I also won't try to take credit for your rock-star status, because it's all on you!) So, now that you know and own your options, here is my favorite approach:

"It's easier to ask for forgiveness than for permission."
- Ralf Manok (My prior boss and one of the good guys)

I am not sure if Ralf borrowed this saying from someone else, but those are the words I've lived by.

They've been compelling enough to make my lizard brain shut up. So, they might work for your lizard brain too.

And now that you know your 3/2-method implementation options when dealing with an employer, let's talk about the next big decision you need to make.

Remote—Or Hybrid?

This question shapes so many of our work choices right now it's hard to know where the answers should start. But let's go ahead and think about the work environment first. While you may not be fully remote, hopefully your employer got the note and offers a hybrid model for you to work (if not, make him read the Owl Lab's report "State of Remote Work"). This is what you need.

How many remote days will be best for you? Basically, as many as you can get. If you can get 4 days out of 5 or even 9 days out of 10, this will obviously give you the most remote time. This is a big way you can improve your productivity. But can we put the 3/2 system in place with as few as 2 remote days per week? And what should you do if you have fewer than 3 remote days per week? Let's talk about the answers to these questions.

The absolute best 2 days to choose for remote work are Tuesday and Wednesday, but Wednesday and

Thursday will also work. There is a reason why this should appeal to your boss. Let's say you have 2 remote days, Tuesday and Wednesday. The way those 2 days fit into the week make your employer feel that you can't take advantage of those workdays being remote. Whereas Mondays and Fridays are often remote days that are frowned upon, because the helicopter bosses think you are just using them to spend long weekends at the beach and are not actually working.

Follow all the rules for batching and pruning from chapter 8 because it is especially important that you streamline any meetings on your 2 remote workdays. Use the rules we have established (more than 2 participants will be there or a superior will be present...) and your bargaining power. If necessary, miss a meeting every now and then (maybe you don't want to miss an important client video call, though). On both days, you'd ideally like to have no, or no more than 1 hour's worth of meetings (and schedule those back-to-back if you can).

With the 3/2 method in mind, I'd like you to plan out your weekly goals as if you only had Monday and Tuesday, followed by Thursday and Friday for work. The total amount of productivity should be comparable to a full week in the office for you. If you hit your goal and get all tasks done by Tuesday evening, you've earned a Wednesday off. This will provide you with the motivation to use your Tuesday efficiently, but also be your measuring guide to ensure you're being fair to the agreement you have with your employers (if it specifies any standard hours).

If your company struggles with remote work, a great book to read or hand your boss is *Remote. Office Not Required* by David Heinemeier Hansson and Jason Fried—they have led a remote company for over a decade now, which means they were doing it long before the pandemic.

And since we're thinking about changing the dynamics of your workplace, maybe we should rewind a bit to go over the things you *shouldn't* have to change before we get further into what the 3/2 method can look like in a workplace that holds traditional 5/2 workweek hours.

What Your Workplace Should Automatically Include

Your job should be measured in clearly defined goals and performance indicators. Remember, you should be working for outcomes, not hours accumulated. And outcomes can be measured in numbers like sales, customer satisfaction, and customer retention rates. If you don't already have a prearranged way for your boss to accurately measure your work performance, make sure to agree on numbers or expectations before starting your 3/2 journey. This is necessary in order for you to have another measuring stick for your performance other than the pure number of hours present.

If your workplace does not offer a tool to hold video conferences, you want to make sure to get yourself a free service (in a 1:1 setting for up to 40 minute-meetings, you can find free tools) or pay for a cheap subscription. This will allow you to hold meetings with your colleagues or clients remotely simply by supplying them with a link they can use to log in from any device at the time of your meeting.

How to Initiate the Conversation With Your Boss

I've created a helpful worksheet that goes along with this section of the book called "Selling the 3/2 to Your Boss—Cheat Sheet". Scan the QR code below to get your copy or go to www.3on2off.com/extras.

So, you've officially decided to make the jump, but now you need to have the discussion with your boss. You aren't alone. I'm going to teach you how to best navigate this talk. Also, make sure to print your worksheet and keep it handy. I promise it will help.

Throughout this book, we have already listed a number of advantages of the 3/2 model specifically, and talked about the flexible working-time model in general. But because it will be easier for you to have this information all in one place, here is a shorthand list of advantages to bring to your discussion:

- If you were brave enough to choose option 3 from earlier in this chapter, have this talk with your boss 8 weeks into your experiment and start by asking about your performance. If it was the same as usual, or better, you should then disclose that you have already been using the 3/2 method.
- Preface how the remote work during COVID-19 lockdowns positively affected your productivity—and mention that you'd like to leverage those possibilities again.
- Assure your boss that you will get the same amount of work done. If they insist on you adding up the same 40 hours, you could offer to work 9 hours and 47 minutes on each of your 3 workdays.
- Remind them that you will be more productive in the long run. While a one-time 60-hour week sounds like a great deal to your boss, any positive results will be short-lived.
- Explain that unlike other employees, you will be able to offer Saturday and Sunday availability during some weekends based on your 3/2 workweek schedule. (It is good to share this especially if you know this has been a point of contention with the company's customers.)
- Blame your move on this book. (Hand them your copy or get them their own 😉.)

And because I want to make sure you are totally prepared for this meeting, here are some concerns your boss might have and ideas of how to solve them:

"Problem" #1: You will work fewer hours than you are paid for.

Solution: If you take the time comparison of the 3/2 workweek to the traditional 5/2 workweek from chapter 5, the number of "missing hours" would only be 4 days per month. Calculated at 8 hours of working time per day, that's 32 hours. If you wanted to offer your boss an equal trade, you'd have to work 1 h hour and 47 minutes longer every workday using the 3/2 method, so a daily hour total of 9 hours 47 minutes per workday would equal the same number of hours you agreed to work in the first place. Since you might be used to longer days anyway already, this could be a trade to use in order to negotiate getting the freedom to work using the 3/2 method.

Also, ask your boss if they'd rather have you spend the full working time, or for you to finish your work ahead of deadlines.

"Problem" #2: Upholding Customer Availability Monday through Friday

Solution: Unless you are a customer-facing service, this availability is not a true 9-to-5 situation, but more for "just in case" circumstances. If you are a bit flexible (as in not saying a forever, hard "No." to having any meetings or taking urgent calls on your off days) you might be more successful in creating a flexible work-time agreement based on the 3/2 model with your boss.

If you are unsure, speak to colleagues about potentially sharing coverage and then come to your meeting with solutions in hand. Your company already needs to find alternatives for you when you are sick or on vacation—how could these same alternatives also work for your 3/2 workday schedule?

I could list a lot more problems, but the biggest one will be your own perception and resulting fear of how your boss will react. There is only one way to find out: Have the discussion!

Parting Thoughts on Shifting to the 3/2 model in a Traditional Workplace

Don't try to bargain for full 3/2 autonomy right away. Maybe your best bet is to settle for 2 remote workdays and position them on Tuesday and Wednesday. Do offer to be flexible if a non-negotiable client or company meeting comes up on your day off. Since the model can be adjusted, you could still shift your weekend to start a day sooner or later (or make it up during your following workweek).

Key Takeaways

- Managers can't tell the difference between who is actually working 80 hours and who is just pretending to.
- It's called work-life-balance. Balance is about a give-and-take—but we have a habit of giving work more weight. As a rule of thumb: if work is allowed to sneak in after 5:00 pm on the regular, work should also sometimes be shortened to end at 4:00 pm or 3:00 pm for personal things.
- There is no requirement for you to work remotely, but if you can get a model with 2 hybrid days, that will help. The best days for those will be Tuesday and Wednesday—which enables you to use the Wednesday-Off model (which we will go over in the next chapter).
- Make sure you have already-established performance markers at your job that you and your boss can use to measure your outcomes so your work doesn't have to be measured in hours alone. Also, make sure you have access to a video tool for meetings.
- Use the Cheat Sheet at (www.3on2off.com/extras) to prepare the talk with your boss.

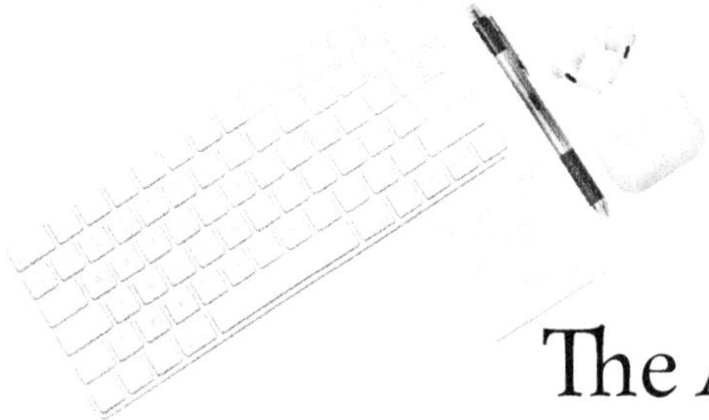

CHAPTER 10

The Alternative Wednesday-Off Model—Fit Your Schedule Within the Traditional 7-Day Week

Time does fly. But you get the be the pilot.

Let's face it: There is one main group of people for whom the revolving 3/2 model is a real challenge: Parents who are bound to the schedules of their kids. Other than homeschooling, there is no way around the fixed timetables schools hold. And weekends are still usually taken up with free-time activities like the ball games that are scheduled on Saturdays and Sundays.

But don't worry. There is still a solution that will help you get the most out of a 3/2 workweek: the Wednesday-Off model. It looks like this: you work Monday and Tuesday, taking Wednesday off, and then working again Thursday and Friday. This way, the fixed days stay the same *and* the 2-day weekend always stays in the same place. So, you're off on Saturday and Sunday. For a glimpse of what a schedule like this would look like, see the chart below.

MON	TUES	WED	THUR	FRI	SAT	SUN
work day 1	work day 2	off	work day 1	work day 2	off	off

The Wednesday-Off Model

Essentially, this is a 4-day week with one day off in the middle, adding up to a total of 8 weekends a month, with half of them being a mini weekend on Wednesday. While the Wednesday off only constitutes a short 24-hour break, some relaxing will still be possible (and is necessary to leverage a high productivity for the next 2 days before the 2-day weekend). The good thing is, this middle weekday lends itself to being your day. Usually there are no ball games, no in-law visits, or grocery runs planned.

So, what does this look like practically? Do you mind if I tell you another story? When I went back to a job where I wasn't the bossv using this 3/2 Wednesday-Off method, I absolutely started to loooooove Wednesdays! More than Saturdays or Sundays. Way more. I wouldn't have thought I could come to appreciate the middle of the week so much. But my partner hated me. Why?

Wednesday had become the day off work that I truly enjoyed myself (and she still had to go to work). In the evening, I would dreamily recount how wonderful having the day to myself had been. But that wasn't how it started.

Before I started using this model I was super reluctant to stop all Wednesday work. *Won't that set me back?* I thought. I did also have a book to finish on top of my other work too (this one!). This thought kept popping into my head: *Don't I have to be busy to be successful?* (The hustle narrative hit me hard.)

Thankfully, I had a concept to test for the book I was writing, so I banished those hustle-culture thoughts from my head. Before I hit "Publish" I had to make sure the advice I was giving out really worked. So, there I was, Tuesday evening, looking at my upcoming Wednesday off and wondering how I could make everything fit into my schedule.

Would my clients accept that all my Wednesdays were blocked from meetings? Would I be able to resist scheduling anything on those days? I needed some kind of reward or incentive that would keep me away from my phone and computer on Wednesdays. At the same time, I knew it had to be something I *wanted* to do—something that maybe I wouldn't allow myself to splurge on otherwise. And that's when I figured out what my carrot would be: indoor climbing.

We had gone before, but the gym was a 40-minute drive away which meant a trip with some relaxed climbing time built in would easily take 3 to 4 hours. This was not the amount of free time we usually had—and especially not on weekends. But I knew myself: if I didn't plan something I'd love to do on my Wednesdays off, I'd eventually slide back into old habits of working.

So, I went climbing on my first Wednesday. And instead of buying a single entry, I bought a 10-pack—and I haven't regretted it. A couple of weeks into my new Wednesday-Off routine, I realized the following: I loved getting up at a decent time so I could enjoy "my day." I also enjoyed doing some housework or things that had be waiting to get done forever. I allowed myself to react on the spur of the moment to finally knock some tasks off my mental to-do list, but never with a plan I had created ahead of time. Hang on, housework? Who likes housework? I swear I never did. And it wasn't something I made mandatory for myself (although it could have been I felt the need to give back a bit to a spouse who had to work Wednesdays).

All the things I did on that day were guided by "I want to" instead of "this needs to get done." If I felt like it, I would do it—otherwise it was "my day" and I didn't feel obligated to do anything. So, if I did decide to throw a load of wash into the machine or clean out the fridge, it was because I enjoyed the feeling after (you know, of not having to look at that dirty stuff).

It was because I looked forward to doing work that didn't require too much thinking while blasting my favorite country music. It felt completely different to do something because "I want to," not because "I have to." Things shifted for me and I started to say things to myself like, "I would like to give 30 minutes of my day away to clean the muck off of our balcony because I know it will bring me and my partner joy."

My Wednesday off was also a great day for me to go and enjoy shops I wouldn't dare set my feet in on the weekend. Full transparency: the Wednesday-Off model would prove to be the most expensive one for me. Because after 2 years of toying with the idea of upping my coffee game, I had time to spend 2 days with an espresso-coffee-machine expert and ended up buying a proper setup. (If you know coffee, you know the sky is the limit, but a decent coffee machine with grinder will cost you at least $1,000 to $1,500.)

Even though my spouse was a bit sour, I didn't let that diminish my feelings each Wednesday night: joy, relaxation, and a sense of accomplishment always washed over me. Also, I wasn't sad in the evening that it was over and I had to work another 2 days. Let's take a look at how this model can do the same thing for you.

	3/2 Workweek	5/2 Workweek	4-Day Workweek	Wed. Off
Work days	18	22	18	18
Days off	12	8	12	12
# of "Weekends"	6	4	4	8

The leveraging point of this system is to plan for 2 mini weeks instead of a 5-day week with an interruption. In addition, it is important to truly unwind and unplug on your Wednesday off in this model. As stated in previous chapters, it is vital to use Wednesday as an off day to recover so you can benefit from the added productivity after this 24-hour break to have the best Thursday and Friday possible.

Since it takes a lot of people a while to "shut down" for their days off, you will have to learn to do this more efficiently for your Wednesday. The tips in chapters 11 and 12 will help you adjust and also advise you on how to get the most out of this midweek day off.

The Wednesday-Off method has the same number of workdays as both the 4-day and the 3/2 workweeks, but has 8 weekends total including the Wednesdays off. That's why this is a great method if you're looking to replace your traditional 5/2 workweek, but there are reasons you can't abandon the 7-day week completely. So, how can you set yourself up for success with the Wednesday-Off model? Let's find out.

Pruning for 2 Days

If you embark on the Wednesday-Off model, you will start by thinking of your week as being 2 workdays. Start and proceed using the same instructions that were described in chapter 8 by marking all the Wednesdays as off days on your calendar.

When you start your workweek, you'll be planning for your first 2 days—sorting the tasks in order of importance and filtering out what you need to get done before your mini weekend and what can be done after. This step is crucial! Don't give into the temptation to plan this as a standard 5/2 workweek with a break in the middle. If you treat it as a normal week, you will relieve the much-needed natural pressure to plan and prune your tasks for 2 days, which will reduce your productivity.

I personally found that planning for only 2 days instead of 3 made my mental tool kit even sharper. Initially I wasn't sure how this would go—since along with the schedule change, I had also just recently moved to a new job. But I resisted the temptation to offer Wednesday as a sacrifice unless it was totally necessary. And this will be crucial for you, too! Just because it feels like you've got a weekend coming anyway, it doesn't mean you should give yourself permission to let work bleed into your free midweek day. The moment you give yourself that option, your ability to prune will reduce drastically.

How to Maintain Focused, Batched Working Hours in the Wednesday-Off Model

When compared to the standard 3/2 model, the Wednesday-Off method has bigger leverage through pruning—but fewer of the naturally meeting- and distraction-free Saturday and Sunday workdays that enable batching, since you keep those as weekends.

In order to make use of some of the batching benefits that would otherwise be lost in the Wednesday-Off approach, at the beginning of the month I want you to pick 8 half days you block off completely from meetings. Those 8 days can be spread out any way you like. For example, you could decide to block off every Thursday, giving you 8 half days. You can decide to block a morning or afternoon here and there or consistently choose Tuesday and Friday mornings. It doesn't matter how you distribute them, as long as you end up with 8 separate 4-hour blocks that you vow to keep completely free from any meetings. If you can, you will plan to not go to the office those days, but to be wherever you can do your most concentrated work.

This enables you to make use of batching that doesn't naturally occur when you adhere to normal week workdays. Much of your success with the Wednesday-Off model will hinge on this—so please take this seriously. If you must, go into your calendar 2 months ahead of time and block off the sections for your batched, focused work. Refuse any requests to join "very important meetings" on your blocked days—but if you really must attend (in person or digitally), the best thing to do is move the full 4-hour block of focused work to another day. You must always make sure you end with a total of 8 batched sessions of focused work per month.

In order to be successful with this model, you

must resist the urge to give your Wednesday back to work—prune drastically so your work fits into the 2 days. As a measure to help you resist "sacrificing" your Wednesday, I encourage you to plan a hobby or activity that you really would thoroughly enjoy—every Wednesday. Buy a 10-pack admission to your favorite spa, or schedule time with a friend from out of town that you will now regularly make the trip to visit. Do something that will not only make you look forward to your Wednesday off, but will also help you resist giving your free day up at the first sight of an "urgent" message.

Stretching the 24-Hour Rule to 39 Hours

In the Wednesday-Off model, I challenge you to go completely off on the Wednesday. This means you will *not* log in to your email account looking for your urgent 24-hour messages. Let's say you last check your email on Tuesday at 5:00 pm before going into your weekend and somebody emails you at 5:30pm. What should you do? Well, you need to ask yourself what the real difference would be from them receiving an answer at or before 5:15 pm on Wednesday and 8:15 am on Thursday.

Yes, the 39-hour response time might have made you jump when you read the title of this section initially. But putting this into practice based on the example I just gave you helps you think about what the real difference would be. Would anything go up in flames? Probably not. And let's not forget, this is the most extreme case. It is more likely that you would get an email on Wednesday between 9:00 am and 10:00 am—and that would be answered by the same time next day!

The other strategies we outlined to implement the 3/2 model still hold true for the Wednesday-Off method and are of equal importance, or even more important. Why? In this model it would be so easy to let yourself slip out of these proven systems. It is vital to streamline your meetings as much as possible. Resist the urge to make workdays longer, and make sure to make time for friends and family so that your work hours are more productive and your work-life balance is where you want it to be.

Key Takeaways

- If something (or usually someone, like kids) makes it impossible for you to shift away from the Monday-through-Friday, 5/2 workweek, the Wednesday-Off model is a great choice.
- Make sure to plan something fun, something you want to do (and look forward to) on your Wednesdays so that you aren't tempted to let work slip back in!

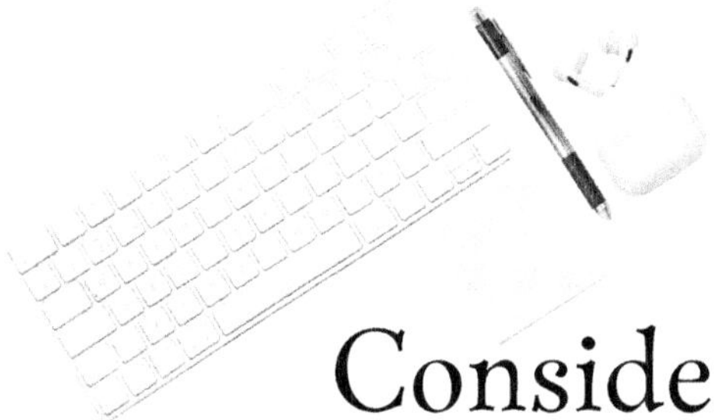

CHAPTER 11

Considerations if You Are a Boss or a Team Leader

Success measured by work accomplished as opposed to hours worked is success that can be consistently replicated.

"What gets measured gets done" is a popular credo in the business world. I'm sure you've heard it. Usually, it is mentioned when a company decides on what benchmarks or measurements to use as marks of success or to fill out employee evaluations. If revenue is a benchmark, employees will target their work to result in higher sales—so an employee will be tempted to sell a customer the most expensive option if they can. If in turn, customer satisfaction is measured with no relation to the sales revenue, employees will be encouraged to sell the option most satisfactory and suitable for each individual client. Even though we only change the one single measure in the same transaction, you can imagine the outcome has the potential to be significantly different.

What result do you get if you measure your employees based on how many hours they work in a standard 40-hour week versus the work they actually accomplish? Let's look at an example of what can happen.

My spouse works in the government where employees are assigned cases. Due to the nature of the work, it is easy to distinguish how long it takes each employee to complete a case, how many cases they have open, and how many they have finished (the closed cases). From January to July, my partner finished between 120 and 130 cases, whereas her coworkers averaged 80 (meaning she completed at least 33% more).

While the length and nature of cases can vary, over this extended time frame, everything seems to average out. With that fact considered, the biggest difference here seems to have been the working speed. Every Monday when the new cases came in, the assigner would look at the open case load of each worker. If they had been productive and had gotten most of their cases done the previous week, their file would show 2 to 3 open cases. Whereas colleagues who had not yet closed older files had 4 to 5 open cases. The assigner then continued to distribute the new cases in a way that assured each person was working the same number of open cases.

So, every week, my spouse would get 2 new cases while her co-workers got either none or 1. My partner would continually get more cases than her peers because she had fewer open cases. Some co-workers intentionally prolonged closing a last case so that their files would show higher caseloads in the system so that they would get assigned fewer additional cases each week. Over months, this added up and the divergence got bigger and bigger.

When we look at this specific example, it becomes clear that this distribution model punishes employees who work faster and more efficiently: They get even more work shoved into their inboxes.

What did you think she did? Let me ask you an even more compelling question: What do you think your best employees will do when they figure out there is no reward for their extra efforts? When instead of a pat on the back and a "leave early today" they get additional assignments? They will start to adapt to the measure you use: The number of working hours spent at work.

After raising the issue of the unfair distribution without resolution, my spouse started to work more slowly and take longer to close her assigned cases. Why? This was the only way she wouldn't continually get assigned progressively more cases than her colleagues.

What do you think will happen if you rewarded your A players for their work by allowing them to keep the free time they just earned by being more effective? The 4-day workweek experiment tells us the result is that you get employees who feel empowered, more committed, and more stimulated by their work.

What world would you rather live in? The 9-to-5, 40-hour week world where everyone is hoping for the five o'clock bell and averting their gaze every time you need someone to volunteer to work a bit longer, or a world where you get stellar work done with the most effective turnaround times completed by happy and fulfilled employees? If you answered the latter option, it's time to rethink how you measure the success of your employees.

How to Shift Work When Multiple Employees Are Involved

If you have decided to implement the 3/2 model with your employees, the first and maybe easiest choice would be to align them all with the same rhythm. That means they will all start working their first 3 days on Monday through Wednesday, taking Thursday and Friday off, and rotating the model going forward. To take full advantage of the 3/2 workweek, I highly suggest you implement a no-meeting/no-email rule for Saturday and Sundays, so that even though they are all on the same schedule, they still get the benefits from deep work and focused time on those days (based on batching).

If this isn't feasible because you are dealing with customers or suppliers that still work 5/2 workweeks and you need at least a part of your staff to be available, there is an alternative team-wide version of the 3/2 workweek to consider. In this case, the 3/2 model can be applied in rotating fashion over a group of employees who are split into X numbers of shift groups (Labeled A through C in the following table). For this to work efficiently, you'd need a minimum of 3 employees. The shift system would become:

MON	TUES	WED	THUR	FRI	SAT	SUN	MON	TUES
Team A Day 1	Team A Day 2	Team A Day 3			Team A Day 1	Team A Day 2	Team A Day 3	
	Team B Day 1	Team B Day 2	Team B Day 3			Team B Day 1	Team B Day 2	Team B Day 3
		Team C Day 1	Team C Day 2	Team C Day 3			Team C Day 1	Team C Day 2

In this shift model, you'd still have a day where the full team is present (or at least all logged in). This day would naturally lend itself to being assigned as a meeting day. I urge you to keep the other days free of meetings as a general rule, as this will enhance the blocks where your employees can get real, focused work done without being interrupted.

Looking At the Real Bottom Line

As we have previously explored the argument that hours do not equal productivity, what is true is that too-long working hours or too many long weeks in a row both pose high risks of detrimental health to employees. This is terrible for a company's bottom line because of absent hours, turnover, and rising health insurance costs.

Even if employers don't care about the well-being of their employees, the extra expenses alone are convincing arguments for shorter workweeks. The longer we work, the more mistakes we make. This is something that the pioneers of the 40-hour workweek (including Ford) learned 100 years ago. It is time to get smarter about using the information we already have.

When in Doubt, Test It Out

If you aren't sure if and how this system will work—test it out like Perpetual Guardian did with the 4-day workweek. Establish some key performance indicators you want to measure before, during, and after your test. Assemble some rules on how this will run (examples being when to hold meetings, when not to expand the working hours per day, etc.) and start testing. The length should be at least 8 weeks, but could be as long as 6 months.

After the decided period, measure the key indicators again and evaluate projects and their successes while asking how the employees felt during the process. Then you'll be able to make your final, informed decision.

Possible Added Choices Via "Freedom Fridays"

You might not be fully convinced that you can make this happen within your company. You might doubt the benefits of this method or be unsure that your employees would buy into it. Here is where the Freedom-Friday model comes in.

The Freedom-Friday model gives you yourself (and your employees) the freedom of choice, while still being able to meet your goals. It also helps you address possible fears (like losing vital workhours). All you need to do is set up a "no meetings on Friday" rule and give clear targets for that day to each employee (hopefully if you've made it this far, you already have clear responsibilities and targets for your employees.).

Then you give your employees the choice. Tell them that they can do whatever they want on Friday. They can either come into the office, or work remotely. They can choose to check their email or not. If they got all their deliverables for the week done and are on target with their goals, they can take the day off and go watch their kid's soccer game without needing special permission. This is the Freedom-Friday method.

If you back this up with an employee satisfaction survey before and 3-4 months after implementation, compare sick days, churn rates, and target achievements, it should give you a pretty good idea whether this method works for your company and your employees.

The reason we choose Friday for this method over Wednesday (which would adhere to the Wednesday-Off model) is that employees only partially step into the pruning and batching benefits. This model has a "see if you get it done or not by that time" approach, which is less stressful for them. This also makes it easier to judge their progress.

It would be more difficult for employees on a Tuesday evening to judge if they could get their week's work done later in the week on Thursday and Friday and still take Wednesday off. The freedom of choice with the Wednesday-Off model is negative because of its non-committal nature. As we have previously explored, one dynamic aspect of the 3/2 model comes through the mental commitment that you have 3 days to get the work done (or 2 in the Wednesday-Off model). This encourages you to prune and batch accordingly so that you are more efficient.

Estimating on Thursday if you got the week's work done according to your goals is much easier to do than overviewing micro-weeks of 2 or 3 days and anticipating how the next batch will go. So, if you want to give involved parties the leisure to choose, stick to Friday for freedom options.

Key Takeaways

- If you are a boss implementing the 3/2 model in your company, you can either schedule all employees based on the same rhythm, or divide them into 3 teams that rotate. You'd still have a day where everyone is working (either in person or remotely) so that you can have team meetings.
- If you are in doubt, give your preferred method a test run. Make sure to accompany it with a satisfaction survey, and measure both the churn rate and days of absence before and after. When comparing those numbers, you should be able to see if the method is working.
- Another good option to give everyone the freedom of choice about whether they work 4 days instead of 5 is to run the Freedom-Fridays method. Give your employees the freedom to do whatever they want on Friday. They can come in, work remotely, or not work at all. If they got all deliverables of the week done and are on target with their goals by the end of their workday on Thursday, they can take the day off and go watch their kid's soccer game.

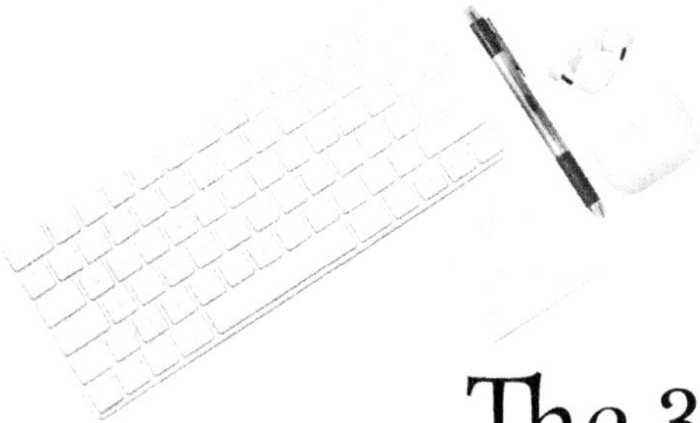

CHAPTER 12

The 3/2 Model in Action

The only way to be sure whether something works is to see it used in real life.

If you've gotten this far and you haven't implemented any of the 3 on, 2 off models or you are struggling to understand how to start, these case studies will help. They are meant to give you an idea of how the different models work for varying roles and show you practical examples that explain how to merge similar positions with the 3/2 workweek successfully. It is my hope that each case study gives you ideas and inspires you with solutions that can solve your specific demands.

Marketing Strategist Patti

Model of choice: Wednesday Off

Job description: Solopreneur who manages all aspects of her business from accounting to client meetings. Next to developing marketing strategies, she builds and writes all of her clients' landing pages and emails. Additionally, she does product support for sales funnel software. Other than attending local networking meetings, all of her work is done remotely and online.

Scheduling or Meeting Restrictions: She already uses a digital scheduling tool where clients book meetings. Other than 2 remote groups she participates in on Tuesday and Thursday, she has free reign over when to schedule what. Most meetings are on an as-needed basis. Only launch periods—especially of corporate customers—might require weekly meetings. These circumstances coupled with the fact she has 2 sons swayed her to pick the Wednesday-Off model.

Pruning: The most important step for this model was to block off all her Wednesdays from client meetings, while moving any that had previously been scheduled to other days.

Batching Strategies: Patti already had certain batching strategies in place, such as bundling client meetings in the middle of the week or doing certain tasks on certain days.

24-Hour Urgencies: In her business, Patti usually responds to emails within 24 hours (on workdays), which is a good time frame she will keep in general. The 2 things she needs to scan for are technical problems, like a landing page or server that has gone down (which hasn't happened in the 3 years she has been doing this) or someone needing software support. To minimize the response time, she chose to add a midday email scan to her Wednesday schedule. For all the other client enquires, Patti will preface her absence on Wednesday and manage the expectations regarding her response time.

Biggest Challenges and Resulting Adjustments: Patti's biggest concern (but also joy) was the question of what to do on her free Wednesdays. She wanted to embrace the urge to take care of household stuff or go places that would normally be full on weekends. We focused on her "I want..." instead of her "I should...." The biggest challenge she faced was resisting the urge to log in and check emails during "off" times in the evening or on her 2-day weekend. She decided not to plan anything on her first few Wednesdays off to see how her "wants" developed.

Conclusion: The first thing Patti noticed was that when she woke up on her Wednesdays, she felt different. Even less rushed than on regular weekend days. This is something the respondents of the 4-day workweek reported too for their Fridays off. While pre-planning and her first Wednesday off still were learning experiences, by her second Wednesday, Patti had successfully limited checking her email. She enjoyed the midweek break and the escape from the regular crowds so much, that on her third Wednesday she took an additional Tuesday off for a midweek getaway with her family (since her boys were on summer break). In the preceding weeks, she also set up several coffee dates on Wednesdays with people she felt she never got around to seeing.

At the time of this writing Patti still continues to use the Wednesdays-Off model successfully.

Remote Personal Trainer

Model of choice: 3 On, 2 Off

Job description: Provides training plans and instructions for people to relieve each client's pain and coach them on how to live a fitter life. In order to make the 3 on, 2 off model more practical, the in-person sessions were reduced and moved to training via video calls. Where possible, the writing and instruction portions were changed to delivery via an app. In the adjusted model, remote clients start with two 30- to 60-minute introductory sessions of direct instruction through video. After that, they have regular video check-ins (once a month or on a case-by-case basis).

Scheduling or Meeting Restrictions: The biggest challenges appeared during video call, 1:1 live trainings with clients. Quite often, clients rely on regular training dates (for example every Monday at 7:00 am) to motivate them to take action. Since the 3 on, 2 off model rotates over a 6-week period, 2 out of 5 weeks, their Monday workouts would be during the trainer's day off and the session would need to be moved to another day. But, by restricting the total amount of these sessions and clients, there is ample room to adjust according to the schedules of both client and trainer.

Pruning: Moving 1:1 services from in-person to remote turned out to be a big enabler for pruning. This meant graduating existing clients into a new service or looking for new clients when certain clients were unwilling to transition. The monthly client meetings are now arranged via online scheduler where each client picks a suitable time. So this didn't become too fragmented, only afternoon slots on Monday through Friday are available regularly. This leaves scheduled workdays during weekends 100% free to do productive work.

Batching Strategies: The few remaining live 1:1 sessions (4 hours a week) get planned back to back on no more than 2 days a week. If no alternative can be found during the trainer's planned workdays, she sets a 1-hour maximum time allowance for virtual training during the needed day off and plans it early in the morning so that it will not interfere with her off-day activities.

24-Hour Urgencies: Her list is limited to the following 2 items: new client inquiries or flare-ups (sudden onsets of pain) of existing clients.

Conclusion: The most stressful components of personal training are the early morning demands and spread-out hours. Most training clients are only available early in the morning and after work in the evening, which leads to a stretched-out day for any in-person personal trainer. By reducing the in-person sessions and moving to a higher share of remote clients, these hours can be condensed. But even if not, the 3/2 method ensures it's only concentrated during a few days, offering sufficient time to rest and recover during days off.

An unexpected advantage of this system has been that it is now easier to accommodate clients with a 6+ hour time difference. Instead of being tempted to have 5 late days, with 3 on and 2 off, work is automatically pruned and concentrated on no more than 3 days. So, in a Monday through Wednesday workweek, Monday and Tuesday would be late days. Compared to the traditional schedule of a personal trainer, this way of working is a lot less stressful. There are also fewer last-minute costly cancellations and revenue drops during time off (because remotely, the training program can be planned even when the trainer is on holiday).

Key Takeaways

- There are ways to adapt the 3/2 method even when tasks and services required vary greatly.
- The best way to address the different challenges that pop up during one's transition to a 3/2 workweek is to choose one particular version of the method and go from there, observing challenges and adjustments along the way.

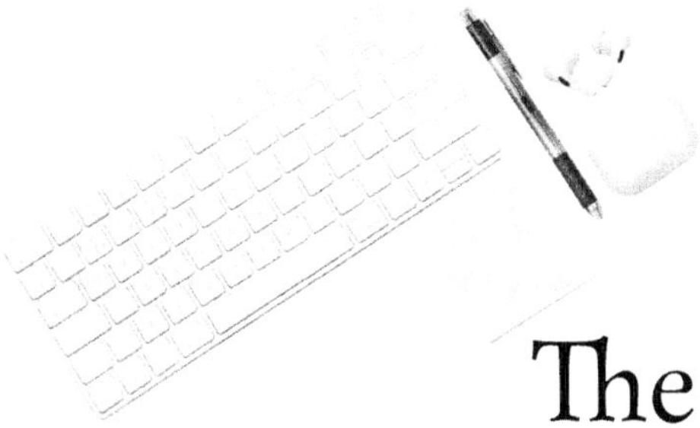

CHAPTER 13

The Power of Breaks and Detachment

All work with no play won't produce high quality work (especially when it comes to remote work).

The rise of remote work opportunities in and after the pandemic has shown to have its benefits, but there are also some major downsides. One of the disadvantages is the lack of physical and spatial boundaries between work and your home (and free time) that are naturally present when you work at a physical office that's not in your house. This point has been illustrated—to our general entertainment and amusement—by the many viral videos during the 2020 lockdown showing news anchors being interrupted by their kids, dogs speaking up on microphones, partners walking in wearing not-so-socially-acceptable attire, and meeting participants showing their relaxed remote state clad in only underwear from the hips down.

Propping up your computer on the dining room table and logging into a meeting within a minute's notice may seem like a great time-saver—but what it does not allow you to do is clearly separate work from free time in a spatial or mental way. How could it? If, from 8:00 am to 5:00 pm, the table is your desk, only to become the center of your family and its meals as soon as you log off, it's hard for your brain to decide if the time spent at the table is for work or for leisure.

The physical boundary of a working space like an office (or a coffee shop you work at) provides a buffer that creates an "out of sight out of mind" response. This internal switch is crucially important for your brain because without it, it becomes difficult to shut off the work part of your life and recover.

You might be tempted to disregard this as psychological nonsense that doesn't apply to your situation, but we have studies that prove the validity of this effect. Plus, I've also experienced firsthand how this phenomenon works. One particular time was during a 24-hour workout fundraiser I held at my gym.

The charity event was designed so that the participants would perform a workout each hour (which could last between 15 and 45 minutes). No sleep was allowed. We decided we needed some seating to sit and rest on in between the workouts, so we moved the lounge sofa into the main training hall right in the corner of the room. The effect it had was immediate: The workout area had previously been visually clean and strictly defined as an area only for working out in. The sofa introduced an aspect of leisure.

During the workouts, I caught myself thinking about how nice it would be to go and sit on the sofa. I don't have to tell you it was a lot harder to stay focused on my workout mode while staring at the soft cushions. I noticed the presence of the couch made it harder not to ease my workout intensity or to take extended breaks. My headspace had shifted noticeably.

This phenomenon is used semester after semester by students who go to the library to study. Most libraries have a culture code that prohibits speaking (or whispering). So, you will find yourself amidst other heads tilting down, concentrated on the books and notes on their desks. This makes it feel easier to study! If you have never seen or experienced this particular group behavior, go do a quick search on YouTube.

You will find "study with me" videos that have 10 million views. You can study with views of Tokyo, or the quiet outskirts of Glasgow, at sunset, or in rainy weather. You can watch a cartoon character or a real person. You can face a zoom call with a group of silent people, or look sideways at someone's laptop and notes on a "nearby" digital desk.

Another occasion that illustrates how your surroundings will affect how you feel and perform happened during the 2020 Spring lockdown when gyms where closed and we ran classes via Zoom—with people logging in from home. Students joined the full hour class from their living rooms, offices, spare rooms, terraces, or any other place where they had enough room.

Many people reported they found it difficult "to get into the workout groove" as their surroundings were either a living room, a kid's room, or right next to the path where their neighbors walked. These things offered mental distractions as well and changed the mindset from "I am here to work out" to "this is where I relax." Some reported they started packing a backpack with their training equipment and moving into the room where they changed before starting the Zoom call to get more "into the zone."

As these stories illustrate, it's hard to get into the zone with other non-related items around if it's the same place that your brain "gets out of the zone." And this is why your dining table which is where you go to eat, connect, and relax with your family doesn't make a productive workspace.

The inability to mentally unplug from work and be fully present during your evenings and weekends, and not be constantly thinking about or triggered over work-related problems, has a direct effect on how you recover and recharge during downtime. And this, in turn, is one of the best reasons to use the 3/2 model (or any working variations of it).

The term "psychological detachment," when discussing work, refers to a state that occurs when people mentally disconnect from job-related issues during their non-work hours. In a related study, results showed that next to a high workload, low spatial work/home boundaries lead to poor psychological detachments from work[63]. Here, we see that this inability to detach from work is again linked to the risk of poor individual well-being. In this situation, one is also exposed to higher burnout rates and lower satisfaction overall[64].

So, in order to be happy, have a well-balanced approach to life, and be in good health, it is important that we not only have control over our total workloads, but that we also create better spatial boundaries and psychological detachment for ourselves, especially when working from home.

If you work where you live, you need to find other ways to separate the 2 types of existence and put some blank space in between them. If you have the liberty, a designated office room (or at least a desk) should be your highest goal.

Alternatively, maybe creating this space requires you to intersect your work start time and end time with corresponding walks (mimicking your commute to work, but also getting in some valuable exercise). You could also drive to your local coffee shop before your workday starts and grab coffee. Maybe you need to pack up your work laptop and stow it away out of sight each evening, only to bring it back out the next day.

Some are even willing to bite the bullet and assign a specified room (or spot in a room) that is only to be used for work, while others go a step further and rent a space at a local co-working facility. Do what you need to do to create as much of a distinction as possible between work time and leisure time. This will enable you to fully "switch off."

> *The idea for Harry Potter came to J.K. Rowling as she was traveling by train and she wasn't prepared. In fact, she didn't even have a pen with her. The question we need to ask now is "Why did inspiration strike when she wasn't working and will inspiration come similarly to us?"*

How Being Away From Your Work Can Help You Make Better Decisions

Where do you get your best ideas? Under the shower? Jogging? A week into your vacation? If you have ever struggled like J.K. Rowling did with a great idea during a time where there was no pen or laptop in sight, you have found the most valuable results of the 3/2 model: the creative, problem-solving power that emerges only during breaks and time off.

There is scientific basis for this phenomenon called the "unconscious thought theory." This theory proves that if you are in need of making a difficult decision, you will come to the best conclusion with a bit of time off as opposed to consciously thinking about it. It is vital to take some time away from the issue if you want the solution to make its way into your mind. Authors Ap Dijksterhuis and Loran Nordgren studied what would happen when people were put into 3 different situations and left to make a difficult decision. Some were exposed to time pressure, others were given ample time, and the third group was given ample time, but laden with distractions that had nothing to do with the decision itself. I'm sure it isn't hard to guess that the third group tended to yield the best decisions[65]. So, it is not just about time away: non related distractions must also be present. Which types of distractions will best support your decision making is a topic we will dive into later.

The important thing here is to understand and trust that the more complex the decision is, the better the outcome will be when approached with enforced time off. If you have ever agreed with the saying "you can't force love," you have found the truth of this concept as well. It works the same. Problem-solving is not about getting up from your desk in this moment and pacing, willing your brain to have the best solution come to you. Instead, it's about creating rest times that allow you to unplug your brain from things you are working on so that when you get back, the good ideas come to you.

But what do you do when even after you rest, inspiration doesn't show up before your next day off?

How to Treat Unfinished Business Until It's Finished

As we have now slowly come to terms with the fact that we will never finish everything or ever be all caught up, there is an important related question we must answer: How do you treat unfinished tasks so that the unconscious thought theory will have its maximum effect during leisure time? We talked about having a designated work place, or visually distinguishing work times from leisure times as an alternative option. But at the end of the day, you must also create mental space between unfinished work tasks if you want your brain to be able to access the "unconscious problem-solving mode" that gets activated by non-work-related distractions.

This can quite literally be you saying "The work is now done for the day. I'll pick up here tomorrow." out loud to yourself. Think of it like the shutdown process that occurs for a computer. At the end of the day, you hit save, close all the programs, and store them away to pick them up the next day. You must resist the temptation to take work issues with you! "I'll think this over tonight so that I might have a better idea tomorrow" does not work. It is better to shut your brain off and let it do its subconscious magic.

You'll also be way less stressed. Dinnertime with your spouse and family feels better when you're not returning to a work issue in your head every 5 minutes. And better time off will allow you to recover and recharge your batteries more efficiently—helping you show up with an unparalleled freshness the next day!

It might feel funny to talk to yourself, informing your brain that you want it to shut off from work, but this will help you express trust in yourself so that you don't keep lingering over work issues during off time. Keep in mind that there will be plenty of time to return to work thoughts the next workday.

It's like meditation. You can't force yourself to not think about anything until you have practiced letting go so that you can return to a non-thinking state. So, how do you practice keeping work issues out of your head when you're no longer at work? Let's find out by taking a look at my childhood in Switzerland.

Ski Slopes and Helicopter Parents

In Switzerland, where I grew up, most children learn to ski at a young age. You usually start out between your parent's legs with them holding on to your shoulders, armpits, or ski suit to keep you upright. Usually, you can tell the level of experience of the kid by the amount of pull the parent exerts on their suit. I often say you can tell which parents have trouble letting go even when their kid is ready by the look on the kid's face. I like to imagine the term "helicopter mom" comes from how those kids look suspended between the groins of their parents—their tiny skis rotating around like helicopter blades.

While it looks funny, it's a great start that helps each kid learn the balance and control that's needed to ski. But unless your parents trust you with more of your own weight so that you do most of your own balancing, you won't ever learn the necessary skills to ski alone. Besides, nobody likes it when their mom is the helicopter, right. When it comes to unfinished work, you need to trust your brain to do the same.

The brain does not work well with orders. If you ever tried forced meditation or demanding that you fall asleep, you know you can't will it into anything. The brain works best with what I call three-dimensional (3D) thoughts: seeing/hearing, feeling, and believing. You can't tell it to shut off if you don't believe that you can better solve an issue after an extended break. If you are subconsciously worried to stop your workday now, the brain will latch onto that worry. Telling yourself (and hearing) that you fully believe you can return to the task and finish it the next day is the key for your brain. You can't outwit it—your brain is hardwired to keep you safe and it will always respond more to what you are truly feeling than what you pretend to feel.

So, as you finish work in the evening, make sure to truly finish work. Plan 10 to 20 minutes each workday to establish end-time rituals that tell your brain the work is now done for the day. And remind yourself not to be like the helicopter parents on the ski slope. You can trust your brain. Let go and trust it to slide through the snow on its own weight to the solution you needed all along.

Don't Work Yourself Into a Rut

Let's discuss burnout for a minute, you know the medical term for a condition that means you've hit empty. Like car batteries, our life batteries don't like being completely drained.

If you feel exhausted and like you need a break you aren't just half-way down the pirate plank dangling above shark waters—you have already stepped into the drop. You're mid-ocean-plunge amidst hungry predators. In the previously mentioned study, Sonnentag and company found that exhausted employees were the ones who struggled the most with disconnecting from work[66]. So, the ones who needed the rest the most were already way past the point of no return. This is a wake-up call for everyone willing themselves "through this busy season," or "the first years of a startup."

You don't have the leisure to wait and just "suck it up"—it might be too late by the time you finally have space to breathe. Plus, chances are that things won't ease up any time soon. We always think they will. We drag ourselves along, powered by the hope of a colorful fantasy—a future time when all our struggles magically disappear. We forget that there is always something else on the list. The next project, emergency, or busy season.

If you are already there, you think you just have to deal with it. But it doesn't have to stay that way. You are reading about how to put the brakes on now. Stop whatever things threaten to derail your capacity—all you need to do is take action to stop the needless actions! And you've got the best tool for it in your hands right now.

To take a page from my trainer background: You don't get better from working out and then pushing even harder directly after. It's not the 100 push-ups that make you more fit, it's the rest and recovery period after them. If I asked you to do 100 and then within a minute of finishing, asked you to do another 10, you would not perform better. Instead, you'd be tired and struggling. But if you wait a day or two to come back, the next 10 (or even 100) would feel a lot easier.

Key Takeaways

- Working from home has a major downside: It erases the spatial boundaries between work hours and free time. We need to find alternatives to log in or log out of work in order to make the most of our non-work hours.

- You can't force anyone to fall in love with you. And it is the same with complex decisions and creativity. The "unconscious thought theory" tells us that you can't sit at your desk, willing the good ideas to come to you. Instead, offer yourself space and time off to rejuvenate and let your brain be bored enough to come up with your next great idea.
- When you finish work, make sure to truly finish work. Plan 10 to 20 minutes to finish up so you can establish rituals that tell your brain the work is now done for the day.
- In Switzerland, most kids learn to ski at a young age by parents straddling them between their legs and skis.
- Just like modern batteries, our mental batteries don't like being depleted to zero. Unfortunately, the people closest or already in a burnout are the people who struggle the most to do anything besides work. To prevent this, it is important to implement breaks and sustainable working techniques long before burnout happens.

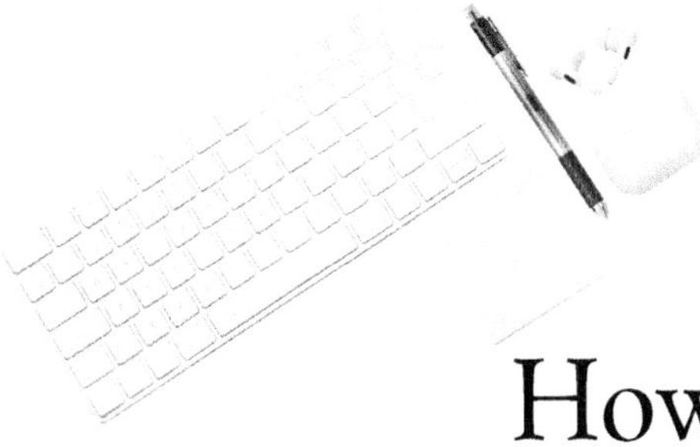

CHAPTER 14

How to Work More Effectively

"If you chase two rabbits, you won't catch either one."
—Russian Proverb

If you haven't yet switched to the 3/2 model because you're still concerned that you might not get everything done, or that you'll underperform and overpromise when it comes to your boss, etc., this chapter is for you. There are numerous productivity books out there, but the good thing is that for the 3/2 model, you don't need a special one. You just need to get out of the way of letting the system do its work.

So here are the most important hang-ups that, if avoided, will give you the needed momentum for the 3/2 method to take your output to the next level. Or, if you aren't ready to take the leap and rearrange your workdays to the 3/2 method, here are some tricks on how to still get more out of your work (remember though, if you work more efficiently, you also earn the right to take more days off).

Prune Seriously—The Power of "No"

The biggest lever you can pull in the 3/2 method system is the power of pruning that happens naturally due to the fewer available days (Monday through Friday) to plan and hold meetings. But part of pruning is also assessing every task to figure out whether it's important enough to make your 3-day list. The external limitation of the available days helps—if you let it.

Your biggest ally will be saying "No." No, to certain obligations. No, to recurring meetings. No, to things "that have always been done this way." As you plan your 2 or 3 days of work, be stern. Only allow important things to survive your pruning. Remember, it's impossible to grow a big pumpkin without pruning away everything but the most important fruit—and that brings us to the next point. It's time to figure out your most important fruit.

Focus on your Most Important Tasks (MITs)

There is a truth every single person has to face: You will never be done with everything. You will never be all the way "caught up." You will never have enough downtime to get all of the projects waiting at home done. It will not "be better once the Christmas run is over" or "the busy season is done." You will never be finished with all your tasks at work. Those are all lies you've been telling yourself so that you can keep going. The truth is, you will come to utter exhaustion trying to chase the moving finish line that has "Everything is Done!" painted across it. But it doesn't have to be that way.

Whether you work using the 3/2 method, a 40-hour workweek, or even a 100-hour workweek, you have to focus on the most important things because you *can't* do everything. (You will run yourself into the ground if you try to.) There is no time frame in life when all of your tasks will be done because new things will continue to pop up on your to-do list. Remember the Parkinson's law? How tasks take as long as the time you have to get them done? This is also true for new tasks that come in. They will always fill the time you have available. If your to-do list is close to empty, you will also be tempted to put more things on the list! The easiest and best thing you can do to be effective while maintaining your mental and emotional health is to face this fact. Now, and multiple times each and every day. Repeat after me: "I will never be done with everything." I mean it, say it out loud. And start saying it each and every day.

This means that several times a day, you need to ask yourself what the most important task on your list is so that you can prioritize it. The 3/2 method helps you do that by making you super aware of the restricted time you have (remember, you don't plan further ahead than 3 days at a time) when you're choosing what to work on.

Each workday, you can better execute this step by writing down your Most Important Tasks (MITs). There have been several methods proposed to do this, ranging from only 1 to 10 most important tasks per day. There's a boardroom campfire-style legend that MITs always remind me of.

Once there was a famous billionaire who was considered to be one of the wisest in all the land. One day, his pilot, knowing of this man's renown, asked him what the secret to success was. In response, the famous passenger asked the pilot to make a list of his top 25 career goals. So, the pilot listened and brought the list to his passenger. The famous business man then gave him a second task, telling the pilot to narrow the list down to 5. When the pilot did this, the billionaire asked the pilot what he would do about the 20 items he had taken off the list. The pilot responded, "They're still important. I'll do them in between the top 5 tasks when I can." The billionaire took the paper out of the pilot's hand and said, "Wrong, these 20 are distractions! They must be avoided at all costs until the 5 most important things are done."

The number of things you should focus on has varied over time. In their book *The ONE Thing*, authors

Keller & Papasan propose that there is only 1 thing at any given time that can be the most important. If you look at what will have the biggest impact that also aligns the best with your values and will keep driving you forward both now and later, there is 1 task that is superior to any other on your list, and that is the one that you should do for yourself right now[67].

So, what I would suggest you do is focus on what I like to call the golden middle, which is made of 3 MITs every workday. If, for some reason, you got a call at lunch that was a real emergency and you had to drop everything—what would have to be done to make today a success? Those 3 things go on your list as MITs. Until they are done, do nothing else. If possible, don't even check your emails (or if you need to due to the 24-hour rule, apply your 24-hour filters and only handle the urgent messages). Your only focus is getting those 3 MITs done as soon as possible.

If you have trouble deciding on just 3, use this question to decide: "What needs to be done by lunch if I need to drop everything I am doing and still be able to come back and keep going tomorrow?" You should be able to get them done by midday, but you must guarantee they will be finished before the end of the day—don't forget there are other things on your schedule, and short-term emergencies might arise. It might take you longer than lunch, because humans are not always good at correctly judging the time required for a task. That's okay. However, it is important for you to have a positive experience so that you are able to say "Yes, I got the most important things done." If you got your time estimation right and you get the MITs done before your workday ends, then here's a bonus: You get to pull out the "other" to-do list out and start a bonus MIT.

Working in Time Blocks

Now that you have your MITs for the day, next you should plan out how you will spend your time. This is probably one of the easiest things to do to guarantee that you will get a major payoff by completing an effective workday. Start by determining what time your day will finish. When do you want to leave the office by? Do you *need* to be finished by a certain time so that you can make your kid's soccer game? Whatever time it is, set your workday to end 15 minutes earlier to give yourself time to pack up. If it's 5:15 pm, your finish time now becomes 5:00 pm.

Now, write that time at the bottom of a piece of paper or on a new page in your journal or daily planner. Then draw several lines above it so that for each 30 minutes you have 1 slot until you reach your start time. This is the total time you have for your workday split up into half-hour blocks. (If this sounds like too much work for you—there are plenty of planners out there, both with and without dates, that already come in this format.)

Now that you see your total available time in one place, you see that you have a lot to work with, right? Now your focus needs to be on using this time efficiently. If you have meetings today, write them down in the according time slots, planning in the time you need to prep the meetings before and maybe to finish up or get the most important related to-dos out of the way afterward.

What you are left with are the available time blocks you have for work. If you haven't picked up on the theme already—pruning meetings down to half an hour and cutting any that aren't necessary are essential steps for a productive day. If you can group those meetings together, even better.

Now that you have written down the things you can't shift on your schedule, you want to find free time slots for your MITs. Block off time for your MITs as soon as possible in the morning (remember, if you had to drop everything at lunch and run, you wouldn't want to have to come back to work later). Start with the most important MIT in the first available slot. When blocking out the time you'll need for that task, plan for a bit of buffer time.

So, if you think it will take you 1 hour, make sure to assign 90 minutes. If you only have a too-short slot to choose from as the first slot of the day, think about what it would look like to at least get a head start. Or, would that slot fit another MIT perfectly? Weigh your options, aiming to get as close as possible to 1 block of time that allows you to finish each task. It is also important to plan them so that all 3 MITs are finished by the end of the day. If you can't accomplish this, you will have to reassess whether you need to cut down the MITs on your list, or if you need to figure out a way to complete them in a shorter period of time than you have available.

It will take you some practice to assign and judge the time correctly for these blocks. At first, there might also be interruptions or distractions, which we will talk about in an upcoming section so you can reduce them. To prevent you from running hours behind and feeling frustrated, plan out some buffer areas in your schedule at various times during the day. (You will also need bathroom and food breaks.)

When planning your blocks, it is best to plan each of them to be at least 1 hour of working in depth on a single subject. Then add more as your schedule allows. It will take you some time to dive fully into each subject to get the most efficiency out of your work time. Here is where the batching from the 3/2 method comes into play: Now you will plan to go through all of your similar tasks in 1 accumulative block. Log into that tool once, whether it's online banking software or a task-managing group calendar, etc. Complete tasks that use similar processes together (do all your scanning, and then all your filing). This will save you time as you harness the power of concentrated, connected thought.

Once you have successfully planned out the day's MITs, you can assign time to anything else. But make sure you start the day by using your task list and nothing else. That includes checking email. This is important: you have already decided that this task is one of the 3 most important ones, so don't get distracted from it. If something else comes in that is extremely urgent, you would need to reassess what your 3 most important tasks are and assign their order of succession.

If you finish the first MIT, make sure you start with the next one. Don't fill in the gap with something that ends up taking more than the time you have. If you finish all of your MITs early, you get to celebrate: Theoretically, after that, you could go home! Any other work counts as a bonus. That's a good feeling, isn't it? That is also one of the reasons I urge you to plan just a few MITs and make sure you get them done well ahead of the end of the workday. So even if something were to happen, you would get them done and earn this small win. Wins will keep you going because they make you feel accomplished and productive. And you will want to come back for more the next day.

Every fitness trainer or life coach in the world will tell you, it is much better to motivate a trainee with small achievable challenges and stacking wins than huge, impossible objectives. Nobody likes to get beaten down and lose every single day. Those people end up quitting. So, creating days you can win at is crucial.

If you misjudge or misplan your day so that you end up either rushing or not finishing your work, it drains you. You will not be exhilarated to come back. You will have trouble shutting off work at the end of the day and this will leave you feeling less refreshed when you come back for your next workday. So, how can you tackle projects that will definitely take more than a day of hitting everything on your MIT list? Let's take a look.

How to Tackle Bigger Projects

Projects that take several subtasks and multiple workdays (or workweeks) pose a unique challenge because there is a temptation to get just enough done before time runs out. You don't want to end up in a deadline sprint like my team with the Easter bunny sale. But when you are comparing a bigger project with your other Most Important Tasks, how do you decide when the project tasks are more urgent than the others?

The best way to strike a balance between long-term projects and short-term goal-related urgency is to divide and conquer. Plan a certain number of hours per week or day that you consistently fill with work on the big project. This can be done in a calculating fashion, where you think about how many hours this project will most likely take (let's assume it will take 50 hours) and split it between the workdays you have between now and the deadline. If the deadline is in 6 weeks, you'll have 18 workdays a month (in the 3/2 workweek model) multiplied by 1.5 months which equals 27 workdays. So, that's 50 hours divided by 27 days, which gives you a quotient that tells you to spend around 2 hours per workday on the project. Or 4 hours every other workday. Or 1 full workday a week.

When you plan your day, these 2 hours will get slotted into your schedule just like your meetings or other fixed points. Only then will you insert the MITs. This guarantees that you keep making progress on your long-term project.

When deciding what to work on during this project's time slot, you'll use the same approach to the pruned time frame you already use: If you only have 2 hours to work on it during that workday, what is the most important thing you need to work on for this project?

I used this big-project time-blocking approach to study for an exam and write this book while still completing all my other work.

Reducing Distractions

If you've ever taken a transatlantic or transpacific flight, you know how long 8 hours can seem. You watch a movie, you eat, you chat—and check the time thinking you must be close, but you aren't even halfway there yet. The 8 hours feel endless! How different 8 hours at work can seem. Some days, you haven't even gotten through your MITs and it's already time to end the workday.

The reason the flight seems longer when compared to a workday is that there are no distractions interrupting you. I know of several authors, journalists, and business professionals who use this unique setting to their advantage to get a lot of work done. There is no incoming email or internet browsing that interrupts work (let's just quickly check what the Dow Jones is doing...). There are no meetings that have a prep time and a tail end. No chatty co-workers stop by. In short: the environment is distraction-free.

What if your 8-hour workday was just as distraction-free as a flight from New York to Paris? How much work could you get done? Unless you want to buy a round trip ticket to Paris (who wants to see the Eiffel Tower anyway) or pay for an expensive hotel while you stay there, you have to find another method to protect your time from distractions in order to get meaningful work done.

Some of the biggest distractions include: Any buzzing notifications (from new emails, signaling incoming messages, your phone ringing, etc.), chatty co-workers, or mindless internet browsing. The constant noise scatters your attention and multitasking or switching tasks frequently combined with unplanned visits to social media platforms (that are literally geared to pulling you in and keeping you for as long as possible) make focused work unimaginable.

The first thing you want to do once your schedule is set, is shut off *all* your notifications except for a 5- to 10-minute warning to alert you of your meetings (of which there should be few left—if you followed the advice from chapter 8). If you struggle to find where the different notifications come from, use the "Do Not Disturb" function that phones and MacOS systems have (it's called "Focus Assist" on PCs). Nothing else should pop up or make a sound on your phone or computer.

The "fear of missing out" (FOMO) is real. But your job is not to stay on top of every developing story (unless of course you are a journalist, and even then, you usually pick one at a time). You won't miss anything important. If your house is burning or the world is finally going belly-up, you will notice—even without your notifications turned off.

Shut Off the Internet (or Batch Internet Times)

The biggest difference between your standard 8-hour workday and the 8-hour flight from New York to Paris is the lack of distraction, mainly in the form of the internet. Arguably, the fastest accelerator of technology in our past century is also one of the biggest time sucks that needs to be avoided if you want to focus your attention on business.

The easiest thing to do is to shut off your internet connection by disabling Wi-Fi, unplugging the modem, or both. This should take care of the email notifications, the pull of funny YouTube videos, click-bait articles about the foods that you should never eat again, and online shops with orders that you just happen to have remembered to take care of in that moment.

There are several tools that you can install on your computer or on your browser that either limit your surfing time or which pages you can look at. For example, you might need access to The New York Times for work, but not other sites. If you need the internet for your work, decide on a batch time when you can do your internet-based work. For example, you could make a rule that you can use your web browser every hour on the hour until a quarter past. But if it is 16 minutes past, your tool will disable access to the internet, preventing you from going down rabbit holes of distraction.

Think about the last example. What if you needed an answer to continue your work at 9:25 am? It's definitely past 9:15 am. In that moment, I would urge you to set aside this task, work on something else, and wait until the time comes around again. In most cases, you will find out that you can either wait or work around the issue until the time comes—or even that it solves itself before that.

In the very few cases, when you can't avoid a

holdup by waiting for the next planned internet time, do the following: Wait for 5 minutes. This is important. Do not succumb to the temptation to skip this small waiting time. This brief pause will teach your system that it does not get immediate gratification—it will not be rewarded for finding a way around the available internet times you have established.

After the 5 minutes have passed, you should start your next internet block. That means, you get the assigned 15 minutes before another 45-minute downtime follows. You should treat this adjustment as merely moving the block ahead. You do not get additional time over the course of the day—instead you have moved it forward and accessed it earlier.

By doing this, you learn to keep working on the meaningful tasks and you learn to resist urges based on instant gratification gained by distractions both big and small.

Long Live Single-Tasking!

I'd be hesitant to name which lie of the last century has had the biggest detrimental effect on our work, but if I had to, it would be this: the manifesto of hustle culture that productivity per hour can be increased through multitasking. "But wait, Linda!" you might say, "Can't a good multitasker do more things at the same time, hence get more done?" The truthful answer (and I will always tell you the truth) is "No."

There is actually no such skill as multitasking, no matter how intelligent or talented you are. Brain scientists have discovered that if you are multitasking, you are in fact switching between different tasks at a high frequency. Effectively, this means you are single-tasking and switching from one task to another.

Our brain does not process multiple things at the same time. A good way to think of this is to write 2 parallel lines on a piece of paper. If you run your finger on one, you can jump from one to the other as you move forward, but you can't run the same finger on both of them at the exact same time (no folding the paper allowed). So, while you might think you are multitasking, you are actually just switching between different tasks in a rapid fashion.

And no matter how rapid you are, you will lose time as you refocus—or you won't be able to dive as deep because you keep switching. Let me give you an example. If you're in a traffic jam and watch the cars that constantly try to switch lanes in order to find the fastest one at any given time, what happens? Are they ever really moving faster than you as you stay in your same lane? For a moment, they might have a small gain, but you'll end up meeting them at the stoplight when you both take the exit.

Only 1 Tab, Browser, or Document at a Time

If we were to look at your computer in the middle of work, how many browsers, tabs, and programs would you have open at the same time? Count every program, every tab in your browser (yes, in every browser window)—What does that add up to? Is it 10? Is it 20?

If you are like me, 2-3 hours into your workday, you've hit 20 or more. Have you ever heard that you should keep your desk clutter-free to limit distractions? It's good advice, right? Why should your browser or computer screen be any different?

Let's think about another example. Let's say in order to do your uninterrupted work, you are checking out co-working spaces or coffee shops. Would you be more likely to work at the crowded campus joint where several 20-somethings are assembling in big noisy groups with all sorts of bikes, scooters, and skateboards while leaning between the coffee tables? Or, would you be more productive at the sleek co-working space based on industrial design with minimal art on the wall and clear, simple desks arranged in neat rows? You know, the one that isn't too busy.

Where could you do more focused work? Just like a busy coffee shop, the presence of 20+ tabs creates 20+ chances for something to catch your eye and pull your attention toward it. And that is the problem with all the tabs. You might not think so, but every item that is open demands a bit of your energy, even if you are not looking at it or working through it actively. (Also, in all honesty, if you have 20 tabs open, the chances that you find the one you need will be significantly reduced.)

So, clean up all the items scattered on your desktop and either delete each item or organize by placing it into its proper folder on your hard drive or in your cloud storage. If you can't do that because it would take up time you don't have, drop everything into a folder (adequately labeled "stuff") that subs as a pre-trash folder (to be cleaned up at the next opportune moment). This will take merely 5 seconds of your time, but will give you added calmness and concentration.

Furthermore, your task from now on (starting today) is to only have the window or tab open that you are currently working on. If you need to look something up or send an email, open that, work on it, and then close it again. Make sure to close the email program after that so you have no chance of seeing the new emails come in (because you shut off your notifications!).

If you are worried you will "lose something," rest assured: Your browser saves your past history. You can check the "keep me logged in" and trust auto-complete will help you remember the web addresses (or you could use bookmarks). Plus, internet load times have become lightning fast—there is no excuse not to close everything and re-open browsers and tabs instead of bogging your computer down with 20+ open tabs.

You are only allowed to have one tab, browser, or program open at the same time. If you are waiting for something to upload, *do not* open another window or tab. Instead, be bored and wait. Because if you jump to the next best thing, it might take you down a social media rabbit hole that swallows up 30 minutes of your time before you realize it.

> *In aviation there is the "sterile cockpit rule": Below 10,000 feet of altitude, no discussions related to anything other than the actual flight are allowed. If distractions aren't limited for pilots, this could prove to be fatal to everyone on the plane.*

Establish Your Own Social Media Rules

Let's be honest, we've all said "I'm going to spend less time mindlessly scrolling through social media" before—maybe you even set up boundaries on your phone in the form of time limits. But all you do is click "Ignore for 15 minutes" and go right back to it. If you don't believe me, go and check the settings of your phone (called "Usage" for iOS or "Digital Wellbeing" for Android) and check your total time spent each day or week on social media.

Let me guess: What you found there was a lot more time spent than you thought!

Of course, if you can do without them, removing all social media tools from your work phone and computer would be best (if you have another iPad or private phone you use only when you are off work). But maybe you do need some tools for work or for business (especially for marketing purposes). So, my proposition is that you establish some rules for your social media use. Through years of self-experimentation, I have found that time limits (even if enforced with a timer) rarely work. If my browsing time was up by midmorning, I would still get on "for just another 15 minutes, I promise!" The timers that are available on phones (enabling you to set a total time limit) are easily overridden with one click. So, unless you are very talented at adulting and holding yourself accountable even when nobody else is watching, this won't be a viable option.

I also tried moving the apps to different places on the phone so I wouldn't habitually find them. That usually lasted about 4 days—by then, my monkey brain had figured out what page they were on and I was right back in my old habit of mindlessly picking up the phone.

Finally, the method I found that worked best was to create rules that are linked to something else that can be clearly defined. I first realized this when I successfully limited my browsing to times spent in the bathroom. (I purposely say "in the bathroom" as opposed to "on the toilet" because then it just became more time spent in the bathroom and had little to do with—well, you know.) But then, I realized I disliked that I would feel the urge to pick up the phone on any occasion I would go to the bathroom—even making sure to take the phone with me when I got up from a conversation to excuse myself—all because I didn't want to miss the then-related social media time. Plus, I was constantly having to explain myself to my spouse and friends who kept asking if I was okay after these extended bathroom breaks. That's when I realized my toilet-phone method wasn't helping me as much as I wanted it to.

If you in turn link your social media time to something that you already do, it becomes easier to stick to it. But maybe attaching this allowance to something you do frequently isn't a good solution. What has worked well for me is to only use the phone during alone meal times. The time preparing the food, eating and lingering after with an espresso are clearly defined. I might prolong it a bit if I get pulled too far into social media, but I have a total time for my lunch break that can't be adjusted, making it a lot harder to overrun my time-budget in a massive way.

With this clear line established, all the additional pick-ups during work time, which can end up in 5- to 30-minute time sucks all over the place, disappear.

Key Takeaways

- Your biggest ally will be saying "No." No, to certain obligations. No, to recurring meetings. No, to things "that have always been done this way."
- Use "Most Important Tasks" (MITs) to figure out which things are most vital to do that day. Make sure you plan those in at the earliest time possible.
- Plan your tasks in time blocks, clearly defining a start and an end time.
- Reduce distractions. Pretend you are on a transatlantic flight. Shut off or limit your internet consumption.
- Establish your own rules for social media to limit your distractions.

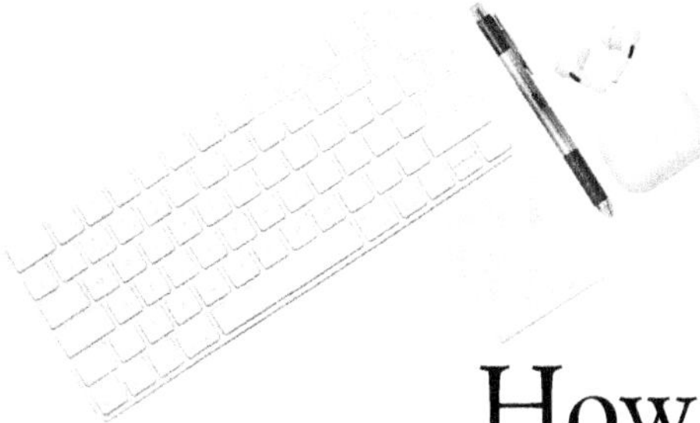

CHAPTER 15

How to Spend Your Free Time

Having a career is not the same thing as having a life.

People often find knowing what to do with their free time hard if they haven't purposely taken time off before—they literally don't know what to do with that work-free time. It's like when someone quits smoking—most smokers don't struggle with the actual lack of cigarettes or even nicotine—but well-established rituals, like smoke breaks or having a cigarette with their beer, now pose a void that needs filling. It is more difficult to work around the void and *not* to pick up a cigarette again than to fill the space with an alternative that keeps one's mind busy.

After juggling between building my own company and my other full-time job, I literally didn't know what to do with myself during my newfound free time. I had essentially worked 2 different jobs spanning 40+

hours each next to one another, and then transitioned into being a full-time entrepreneur working 90+ hours a week. There was no leftover space for free time activities—not that I would have remembered any.

In the past, all I knew was getting up at the crack of dawn, eating a quick breakfast, going to work, coming home at 9:00 or 10:00 pm, eating, and finally, falling into bed exhausted—just to repeat it all over again the next day. On weekends, I would get an additional 2 hours of sleep in and maybe finish work by 5:00 or 6:00 pm—with no energy left to do anything major. If I had any free time, I worked out (this was the one good thing from that season).

After 5+ years of living that way, I had very few friends left since I never had time to call them. I missed all their social gatherings and big events because I was always working (and with time, people learned not to invite me in the first place). My relationships had dwindled. I kept saying "I'll see you if we have time for an hour this weekend," but that hour never came.

I had no hobbies outside of my workplace (working out as a hobby in the place that you own and run is usually split between actually working out and tidying up or fixing things you see). The sparse time I had left was spent every other week on basic house cleaning that wouldn't pass either a mom or mother-in-law test. And then, there were extension periods for taxes to apply for, bills to pay, and other things I had neglected in order to churn out those insane work hours.

As a direct consequence—even if I had had time for anything besides work, either I didn't know what to do, or I was too tired. My life was a mess, and I was a mess. The only thing preventing me from complete burnout was that I didn't know how to afford that time luxury so that I could allow myself to have a full breakdown.

So, I get it if you are looking at the page wide-eyed, wondering what you would do with all the hours outside of work (which is 32 hours a week with the 3/2 model). Let me tell you, this is one of those chicken and egg problems—it's hard to agree fully on what comes first. It could be that you don't know what to do, but you also know that you don't have the time for anything other than work (or family). But don't worry, we will find you a hobby—something to do. The goal is to keep you from being bored, or—worse—using the time for work again just because you don't know what else to do.

The Power of Inherently Fascinating Stimuli

So, what is your best choice when it comes to filling your breaks and downtime? What if you could stop working long enough to actually refill your batteries? Let's start with something that science has shown to be the most productivity-enhancing.

Would you ever think it could be something as

simple as spending time outside in nature? The attention restoration theory, first proposed in the 1980s by Rachel and Stephen Kaplan, states that spending time in nature or just looking at nature has the power to restore concentration[68]. Since then, this has been tested in several environments and situations that give us important clues about which breaks are powerful and help us recharge better.

For example, after walking through a busy city center you will be less likely to concentrate than if you had walked through nature. Having to pay attention to small things in the city is distracting enough to keep draining your capacity for concentration. Looking for red lights or pedestrians crossing your path uses the same "system" of the brain that you need for critical thinking or concentrated work.

Similarly, just switching screens during your break and scrolling through your phone will *not* help you recharge. Our eyes are magnificent tools that can change focal lengths from objects close to far away—keeping a phone at a fixed distance is actually tiring and creates additional eye strain. So, it's better to get out and get away from screens.

Walking in nature offers sufficient enough stimuli that your brain is occupied, but can recharge instead of being drained. If you're in doubt, start with walking for an hour outdoors. Walking also offers another benefit which we will get to in a bit: It's a form of exercise.

The Best Activities to Recharge

When they looked at which activities caused the best opportunities for recharging, researchers found that social, physical, and creative interests are the top 3 choices[69]. Sadly (or should I say luckily?), low-effort activities like housework did not offer the same advantages. So just having time off (and trying to catch up with light activities or your household chores) will not offer the same benefits as going out into nature.

Resource-consuming activities that involve too much of your efforts will prevent your recovery and recharge. Cleaning your house and doing your taxes, or spending most of the weekend shuttling noisy and grumpy kids around will not add to your recovery or make you ready to hit the ground running on your next workday.

Two good activity choices for a break in work are:

- Going for a walk out in nature alone or with your co-workers
- A midday workout

But even smaller breaks where you get up and out of your chair to do some mobilizing exercises will help.

You might be thinking "But wait, I don't have time to plan a recharging activity. And even if I did, what I really need is rest." I've been there: If you are just coming off a long day or a longer spell of working more than 40 hours per week, you might find that it is hard to collect the energy to do anything other than lie on the couch. This is a proven phenomenon[70] which should be your sign to take action as soon as possible.

As ironic as it is, the more you need the recharging activities, the less likely you are to have enough energy left to start pursuing them. Can you see the one-way street we have just entered here? So, how can you get over this speed bump? There's a method to thinking through this challenge that can change everything. I want you to try to remember the last time a new employee or co-worker was supposed to take over some of your work.

Each time I hired an employee to take a task off my plate as a business owner, it took extra work to fill them in on how things were done at our place. In the first days or weeks, any task I entrusted them with could've been done much faster by me. It took time for me to both teach them how to do that task, and to address mistakes they made after the fact. But I knew that if I invested the time in them at the beginning, eventually we would get to a place where they could fulfill the task flawlessly without my help. And then, I would have regained my time. It's the same with me forcing you to take days off. It seems like a nuisance (and lost time) now, but I promise you you'll reap benefits from it down the road.

And to make sure you are not just bored (though some boredom and being able to sit with your own thoughts is good), we'll want to find you a new hobby or have you re-engage in an old one. Because if you are used to working long hours and have no hobbies—if you don't purposely fill that void with something new—you will probably slide back into old habits. Plus, it is more difficult to end your work on time or take the day off when you have nothing nice to look forward to doing.

How to Choose Your Hobby

If you don't have something that immediately popped into your head (like "Oh, I can finally grow that garden") when you read the title of this chapter, don't worry. Your next goal will be to find a hobby that you can enjoy during your free time.

A hobby is, by definition, any activity you do for pleasure in your off time. "Pleasure" and "off time" are important nouns to remember when you are trying to find something new to add to your routine. Ideally, your hobby should have nothing to do with your work or your kids (coaching their soccer team doesn't count as a hobby). It also shouldn't involve household chores. And don't choose something that you think will improve your performance at work. While you can pursue an activity to better yourself or learn something new, this should not be your only motivation.

The most important thing to remember when choosing your hobby is that it must bring you joy.

It should not be attached to any future advantage or learning curve. Yes, it should be as simple as having fun. Give yourself permission to do something just because it fills your cup. This does not have to have an end goal. It does not have to be rigidly planned. You don't need to add it to your calendar as a 2-hour, twice-a-week activity aimed to get you to the next level by the end of the year. You already have enough of that going on in your professional life. Remember, you need a different type of stimulus. Inherently fascinating or creative hobbies can help you recharge a lot better for your next workdays.

Dolce far niente: The Sweetness of Doing Nothing

No, *dolce far niente* is not an Italian dessert, it's a way of life that is practiced in the country of the best desserts. You can fight me about it, but homemade tiramisu and panna cotta are opportunities you should never let pass you by!) Your hobby can be like the dessert that takes the great meal of your life (of a 3 on, 2 off rhythm) to the next level. You too can learn to both enjoy and fully embrace the sweetness of doing nothing. This can be nothing short of your best step to mastering the work-life balance.

One obstacle you might face is that it may be difficult for you to let go of the notion that doing nothing is only for the lazy or the unimaginably rich.

For decades, voices in hustle culture have tried to make us believe that no good thing can come from doing nothing. The lie is that we need to be busy at all times. Plus, there are also always things we will miss. No wonder the acronym FOMO is more familiar to you than *dolce far niente*. But let's change that, starting now.

There is not one concept alone that can describe what *dolce far niente* entails. It is actually so much ingrained in the Italian psyche and way of life, that it is not even an explicit term used in their daily language. It is built into many things they do, both at work and in their free time. It might describe a low-paced summer evening spent at the *piazza* (town center) enjoying company, food, and drink while people-watching. It could also describe a stroll through local nature, without any specific goal in mind or phone in hand.

Dolce far niente means stopping to smell the flowers. It can be just laying on your couch, spending time alone with your thoughts. It can be the steady, deliberate and non-rushed way of working that the Italians have mastered. It is exemplified by the ability and aptitude of a restaurant owner to go over to a random guest and enjoy a glass of wine with them. Or the non-rushed lunch breaks every employee enjoys. Not to mention the general Italian mealtimes that seem to last forever and are totally free from rush. Did you know that there are no early bird dinners in Italy? Usually if you reserve a table, it is reserved for your party until the restaurant closes because the meal is secondary: the most important thing about mealtimes in Italy is the time you spend together.

While it might sound simple to allow yourself to indulge in the sweetness of doing nothing, for those of us recovering from hustle culture, it can mean being willing to sit motionless, in discomfort, alone with your thoughts. When you start on your nothingness journey, it might help to carry a notepad with you so you can dump thoughts out on the pad before a torrent of open-ended, work-related questions sweep away your serenity.

Nothingness can mean that instead of breaking out your phone to document special moments, you just sit there enjoying them with the goal of etching them into your brain's memory, and not your phone's. Discover the art of being in the moment and appreciating life, instead of always trying to create something else to do.

Dolce far niente is about slowing down, enjoying the little things each day and not waiting for the weekend or your next vacation to be happy while you listen to birds sing. It's a sweet mix of mindfulness—doing things you enjoy and enjoying things you do. So, if you don't have all your free time planned out just yet don't worry: Practice filling your cup with the sweetness of doing nothing.

Key Takeaways

- Our brains like a mix of light distraction and some stimulation to recharge. A walk in nature provides both, while a walk down a busy street will not because it takes too much concentration.
- The best activities to recharge are social, physical, and creative.
- Taking off more days a month might seem scary and impossible to you at first—but the rewards will come later. It is important to find a hobby to fill your free-time void so you don't slide back into the old habit of working too many hours.
- Italy has the greatest desserts on earth, starting with tiramisu. They also have a pretty great concept called *dolce far niente*: the sweetness of doing nothing. It's the pinnacle of work-life balance and is a courageous hero standing against the villain that is hustle culture. It's centered on the ability to slow down and enjoy the small things in life every day.

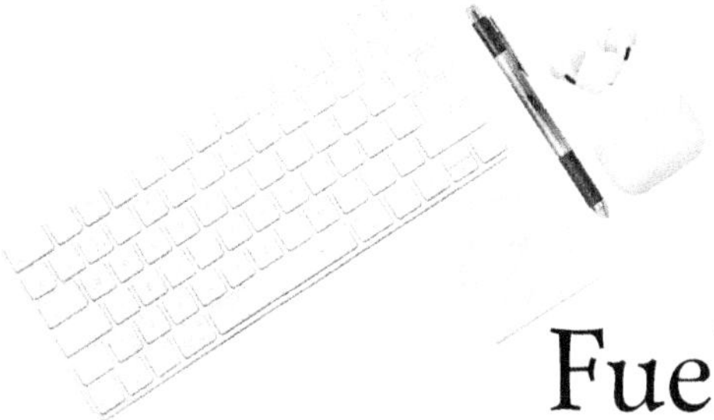

CHAPTER 16

Fueling Your Body & Mind

The best training plan or session can be destroyed with a bad approach to nutrition, a lack of sleep, or a boatload of stress.

We've already discussed what you can do about your work, your tasks, and your daily organization to get more done. An optimal course has been mapped out for your race. You've studied the curves; you know where to break and where to speed up. Sounds like you are ready to hit the racetrack, right?

But wait, you haven't picked your race car yet. It seems like this is one of the most important steps, too. Would you rather have a well-serviced Ferrari, or a rusty-looking and sounding Volkswagen? Yes, your choice comes in red. (Because obviously the Ferrari can go faster. Sorry, VW Beetle fans, we love Herbie, but we have to pick the car that's going to win.)

After you have successfully optimized your work and concentration based on what is best for your mind, we need to look at how you can get your body to perform like that Ferrari. So, what needs to happen?

Your body lives from the way you use it, refuel it, and service or rest it: Everything is based on movement, nutrition, and sleep. What you do in regards to each of those 3 items will ultimately decide if your body races like a Ferrari or crawls like a rusty Volkswagen.

Let's start with the movement part. You'll need a mix of low intensity action combined with high intensity, quick movements (and they shouldn't be done close together). Let's start with the slower movement, which is basically just moving about.

For most of us, this does not break a sweat or take extra special planning. But this is something we lost when we got sedentary and started working with computers as opposed to working out in the field. So, we need to replace that movement to some degree. We've touched on the subject of a leisure walk in nature being one of the best things to restore your concentration and attention. But low-level movement, walking in particular, does so much for you: the benefits move past just giving your mind rest. This low-intensity action is the first staple in ensuring you create more productive days.

10,000 Steps a Day Isn't the Only Way

Ever since the advent of step-counters, the magic number has been 10,000 steps a day. Even the World Health Organization (WHO) recommends this. In fact, it is often the standard goal that comes set for any step counter, smartwatch, or other activity tracker. But 10,000 is not a number backed by research. It is likely that it was chosen just because it's a "pretty number" the marketing gurus established, and has now been accepted without question. It probably originated from the name of a Japanese pedometer sold in 1965 by Yamasa Clock and Instrument Company called *Manpo-Kei*, which translates to "the 10,000 step meter."[71]

You do not have to get to 10,000 steps a day for walking to be worth your effort. Basically, any number will help. Research shows that a daily total of 7,500 steps can lead to a decrease in mortality[72]. For any number above 7,500, the advantages tend to level off[Ibid]. So, substantially more steps will not get you substantially more benefits.

From an effectiveness standpoint, that means you should try to walk between 7,500 and 8,500 steps per day. This will allow you to reap all the benefits of the motion without having to invest extra time. It doesn't matter if it's done in one big chunk or in pieces. Find what works best for you so that you can consistently hit your numbers—on workdays or not.

When I switched to remote work from home, the

biggest change I noticed was a massive drop in my daily steps. At a physical work location, these daily steps had accumulated by me walking from the car park to the office, to the bathroom one flight up, and to the coffee machine in the break room. It was great to have my own personal printer right next to me—but that also meant I couldn't get my steps in. The little things do add up! The amount it had added up to surprised even me, someone who teaches people to move and exercise.

So, working remotely, you might have to plan a brisk morning walk before you start work or during your lunch break. Or set an hourly alarm. I have even seen people set up a walking desk—a standing desk over a treadmill—so they can take their calls while walking.

Alternatively, you could also get a dog (if you aren't allergic). Those who own dogs are reportedly linked to an average of over 19 minutes more of physical activity outdoors and over 1,700 additional steps versus people without dogs[73]. Also, dogs rock as general companions and are good reasons to stop working at decent hours and to go outside at any weather conditions (yes, I'm a dog mom).

But aside from getting a furry best friend, there are also focused moments of action you can take each day to get your step number in the sweet spot.

Ideas to increase your steps/low-level movement:

- Take calls on a walk outside or standing at your desk.
- Plan multiple breaks during the day and get up and walk.
- Use the printer on the far side of your building.
- Get off one bus/subway stop earlier and walk the rest of the way.
- Park farther away from your grocery store. Purposely make more trips when carrying things in to your house.
- Walk to locations that are less than a mile away.
- Walk to lunch and back or walk during your lunch.
- Listen to audiobooks while you walk so you have something special to look forward to.
- Get a dog who needs and likes to go outside (even in rough weather).

Exercise

When I use the word "exercise," I'm referring to anything that is above your regular daily movement. Next to the low-level walking, you need action that is higher-level, meaning it makes you sweat and puff actively (if brisk walking does that for you, it counts as exercise, otherwise, read on). Before we get too much into exercise, I want to talk about intensity.

I've separated the step-count section from the exercise section of this chapter intentionally because you need both. You can't do just one. And you can't compensate for a weaker side by doing more on the other side: You can't walk 15,000 steps a day in hopes that this will get you out of exercising.

What's the best exercise for you? (I bet you've always wanted to ask a fitness trainer that question!) The answer will surprise you: It is the activity you know you will do consistently 2 to 3 times a week for the next 2 to 3 years, and then 2 to 3 decades. Whatever that is for you is right. If you break a sweat, it's good for you. After accompanying more than 2,000 individuals on their health and fitness journeys, I can tell you the single biggest factor to consistency, the kind that has you coming back after holidays or other breaks, is that it is *fun* for you. You have to find the unique activity that is fun to you. Whether it's yoga, Pilates, running, or weightlifting—anything can work. And doing something is always better than doing nothing.

Health wise, it's increasingly beneficial if you include muscle-strengthening activities on 2 or more days a week. So, if your most favorite thing is running, you'll have to think about how to get some strength work in. In most cases, yoga and Pilates include some strength work.

Now that you have that squared away, let's talk motivation: Even if you find an exercise that is fun for you, that does *not* mean that every day you will wake up ecstatic to go work out. You are guaranteed to have days when you feel off. I'll tell you a secret: Even the "pros" in the game have days when they don't feel like sweating. But if it is fun for you most of the time, or at least during or after, it's a good workout option for you.

In terms of consistency, it is better for you to average 2 x 60 minutes of workouts a week than to be the guy who shows up daily from January to May, but goes MIA between summer and Christmas. In terms of how much, the WHO recommendation for adults between 18 and 65 years old is to do at least 150-300 minutes per week of moderate-intensity activity or at least 75-150 of higher-intensity activity. Any combination works as well. The only rule is, if you sit more, you need more. This means the remote computer worker needs more than your gardener or hair dresser (who works standing up).

So, if you work out for 50 minutes at a moderate intensity (up to 70-75% of your heart rate), you need 3 sessions a week. What might that look like? Here are a few ideas for you:

Sample "Ideal" Exercise Weeks—A Cheat Sheet

- 3 workouts of 50min a week. Two strength-, one cardio-based sessions.
- 2 CrossFit™ classes a week, plus 1 moderate-intensity 50min session.
- 2 runs at various tempos (30-60min), 2 strength sessions a week (averaging 45min).
- If you are over 65 years old, include 3 sessions a week with an emphasis on functional balance.

If you are just getting started, start slow and increase the frequency, intensity, and duration over time.

Nutrition

Let me reveal a secret the fitness and health industry keeps from you: You cannot outwork a crappy diet. You can't negate the effect of the 3 donuts you splurged on by doing an extra half hour on the treadmill tonight—even if the calories you ate and the ones you burn leveled out. And most of the time they don't: Depending on the donut and your workout intensity, you could be spending anywhere from 1.5 to 6 hours on that treadmill!

You shouldn't work out to justify eating. You should eat in a way that supports your lifestyle and your ability to work out, and, as a result, enhances your productivity. Also, you shouldn't punish yourself with a workout when you've splurged on a donut. This is problematic because, inherently, if you start using exercise as punishment, your brain will not believe you when you say exercise is fun. Remember, fun is the one thing we need for consistency.

As a fitness and nutrition coach with over a decade of experience, I know I could write my own book about good nutrition choices to add to the 10,000 that are already out there. Actually, I could write a new nutrition book every year, just to address the newest trend, but the thing is: We can't reinvent or discover anything new about nutrition that our grandparents didn't know. So, I will make this short while still trying to give you actionable items.

Eating a balanced, whole-food diet with limited sugar and processed foods is still your best bet. If you've ever gone out to eat a ton of pizza or pasta for lunch, I am sure you were rewarded with an afternoon slump. Many of my clients just assumed the afternoon slump was a natural thing. It's only after I helped them make some alterations to their diets that they realized this is not something you just have to live with. It's a result of the kinds of foods a person eats.

The best and simplest thing I've ever heard was when Dan John, a strength and conditioning coach and author said: "Just eat like an adult." If the packaging is bright and lures you in with loads of marketing and labels that swear what's inside is healthy, it's probably not good for you. (Have you ever seen an ingredient list on a stem of broccoli? Or a funny cartoon printed on the strawberry basket?)

Too many extra pounds on your body make you both physically slower and more tired, but there is also a mental cost. It doesn't matter if you're a vegan, part of the Keto diet, or any other eating method that is highly popular as you're reading this book—each one can work as long as your total calories in versus your calories expended equals out. But what about the donut?

Let's get back to that—I need you to know that I do

not hate donuts. And neither should you. Every food can have a place in a balanced diet. And so should the delightful donut. Or your grandma's casserole. Or your best friend's wedding cake. Here is a saying I love that will help you reframe your approach to food:

It doesn't matter so much what you eat between Christmas and New Year's Eve. It matters what you eat between New Year's Eve and Christmas.

The important thing is consistency. Good, consistent habits let you have some splurges. I don't love the term "cheat day," because it communicates to your brain that you are cheating at something. Cheating usually is bad (whether it's your insurance cheating you in the fine print, or someone cheating on their spouse). Everything should be balanced.

You need things that allow you to live and enjoy your life while going after your goals. Just like when thinking about the work-life balance, make sure that if the donut side gets some love, you'll balance it out on the broccoli side. A good ratio is to shoot for healthy food 90% of the time. Does that sound horrible? Well, it isn't if you do the numbers.

Let's say you eat 3 square meals and 2 snacks a day, that means you have a total of 35 meals and snacks per week altogether. Missing 10% of them would mean 3 to 4 meals. You can do the same for only main meals (which equal 21 total meals per week). With our 10%

approach, you get 2 meals a week that can be all over the place. That's totally manageable, right? And now it's time to talk about the third part of making sure your body is operating like a Ferrari instead of a VW Bug: your time in the garage.

Sleep

Now that we've covered the basics of where you need to put some work in, we get to the wonder drug, the quick fix, the free and easy performance booster: sleep. Adequate amounts of sleep can lower the risks associated with high blood pressure, heart disease, mental illness, and dementia. People who get enough sleep are less likely to get sick from viral infections and are less prone to obesity[74].

The ideal sleep amount for adults is 7 to 8 hours per night. Anything below 7 hours is linked to higher all-cause mortality, higher risk of incident cardiovascular heart disease (plus a 7% increase for every hour of sleep fewer), higher chances of type 2 diabetes, incident depression, cognitive disorders, risks of falls, accidents and injuries, and incident obesity (which increases to 38% if you sleep fewer than 6 hours per day)[75].

So, the real question is: Why aren't we all sleeping more? Why hasn't sleep been heralded as the wonder drug it is? Unfortunately, it is not marketable—it's free. And it also clashes with our hustle culture, because if you work 12 to 14 hours a day, need 1 hour to commute, 1 hour for personal hygiene, 1 hour for household chores, and 1 hour to eat—there is no way you can get 8 hours of sleep. And even then, we haven't thrown in time for getting your steps or workout in, or any social time with friends and family.

For well over a decade, I thought sleep didn't fit into the hustle culture I wanted so desperately to belong to. I was juggling a startup and a full-time job next to each other, and the newest fad was to wake up and be at your desk by 4:30 am. I thought it was working. It seemed like I was performing well with my 5 to 6 hours of shut-eye, and I made it a point to catch up on a couple of hours on weekends. It was only years later when I decided I'd make sleep more of a priority and got a consistent 8 hours a night, that I saw the difference sufficient sleep can really make.

It felt like when you've been wearing old glasses with an outdated prescription for years: You don't realize the world isn't normally so blurry. But then you update your glasses and *everything* looks so different—and so much better. It was the same for me. Around the 4-week mark of getting the 8 hours of sleep consistently, I was falling asleep more easily and earlier (where at the beginning of trying to get 8 hours, I struggled to fall asleep even if I tried to go to bed early).

And I was waking up refreshed, no longer wanting to kill my alarm or anything else that confronted me before my first coffee. But the biggest change was the amount of "brain fog" the additional sleeping hours cleared out. A fog I hadn't even recognized was there. This was especially true around the times I had struggled to feel energy before getting good rest: late morning hours, the afternoon slump, or late evening pushes (which started to become super rare). I had access to quicker ideas for my work and got the work done faster too.

Do you have trouble sleeping or falling asleep? Here are some things to know so you can get improved rest. Sleep is not an event that happens at a certain point of time, like when you switch off a light. In order for us to fall asleep and get a good night's rest, it takes a prep time of around 2 hours—and our body likes to prep us around the same time every night. This relates to the circadian rhythm, which governs the rise and fall of our day and the release of multiple hormones. In fact, for the best sleep you can get, you'll ideally start prepping as soon as you get up.

Our circadian rhythm runs on a 24-hour and 11-minute clock. The implication of this is that your body needs to constantly recalibrate its own inner clock down to match the 24 hours we run our days by. It does so through external things like the time you usually get up, bright midday light, and lower light during sunset.

The truth is, a lot of modern things have wreaked havoc with that cycle: We get up and go to bed at different times during the week and on weekends. We have artificial light to keep us up way past sunset. We spend most of our days inside, exposed to artificial light on screens. So, if your body has trouble falling asleep or staying asleep, the reason is that it is confused as to how you want it to run this rhythm.

To get a better understanding of how this system operates and how we can better prepare ourselves for sleep, let's take a look at the different parts of each day.

Early Morning

To improve your sleep, you need to start thinking about your routine way before you switch off your light at night. In fact, high-quality sleep begins with switching on your light in the morning. Early morning sun and natural light exposure is the first signal to your body that the day has started. Throw open those curtains (in the winter if it's still dark, switch on bright lights). Consider getting some fresh air before your morning coffee for that direct sunlight.

In fact, you'll want to hold off a bit with that first bolt of caffeine. Because if you rely on caffeine to wake you up, so will your body over time. You'll circumvent the natural hormonal cycle that wakes you up in the morning, and your body will get lazy and just wait for the caffeine to hit.

Midday

You should also plan for bright light exposure in the middle of the day. The body has a way of interpreting the angle of the sun rays and aligning the middle of the day with that part of one's circadian rhythm. In the middle of the day is also a great time to exercise if you haven't done so already. Exercising will also increase your ability to sleep, unless you do it too late in the day.

Afternoon and Evening

The first thing you should limit in the afternoon is your caffeine consumption. Caffeine has a half-life of 6 hours, meaning that in 6 hours, half of the 170mg of caffeine that was in your cup of brewed coffee (or 65mg of caffeine in an espresso shot, or a whopping 240-280mg in a cup of cold brew) is still present in the body. So, if you want to make sure most of that caffeine and its effects are gone by the time you go to bed at 10:00 pm, you should stop drinking caffeinated drinks at 1:00 pm.

The last 2 hours of your day are the most crucial when it comes to your future sleep quality. You want to make sure to wind down, avoid screens with artificial blue light, and stay away from exercising. Since our body temperatures change overnight, a hot shower or bath before bed followed by a cold bedroom (64°F/18°C) can be beneficial.

But the biggest thing you need for adequate sleep is consistency. (Are you tired of me tooting my horn yet?) Consistent go-to-sleep and wake-up times should be maintained whether it is the weekend or a workday. I get it, you want to enjoy your social time on Friday and Saturday evenings and then sleep in to catch up on sleep, but what you are actually creating is mini jetlag. It is not unusual for you to throw your body off by 1 or 2 hours each weekend, which is substantial.

Get the "Better Sleep—A Cheatsheet" here:

Key Takeaways

- The reason we even talk about exercise, nutrition, and sleep is that those factors decide if you can put this book to use in a Ferrari, or a VW Beetle. Both are fun cars and will get you there—but if you are looking to get the extra "umph!" of a Ferrari out of your body, you should consider these factors.

- Your body thrives with 2 types of movement: Low intensity for longer periods, and higher intensity for shorter ones. (Both are required.)
- Marketing likes shiny things to catch your attention, and 10,000 steps was such a thing—if you get 7,500-8,500 steps in per day, that's plenty.
- In terms of exercise (anything that makes you sweat), aim for 150-300 minutes a week at moderate intensity, if high intensity rocks your boat, 75-150 minutes is enough.
- If you want to get good sleep, start in the morning. Since your body runs on a circadian rhythm, you want to expose it to bright light first thing in the morning and also at noon—but limit the blue lights emitted from screens at least 2 hours before bedtime.

CHAPTER 17

Making Your Job More Asynchronous (and Remote)

You can absolutely make your non-3/2 method job more 3/2.

Before starting my journey with the 3/2 model, I had one of the most in-person jobs you can imagine: personal trainer and group coach. The fitness business has traditionally been brick-and-mortar. There are 5 major types of support a personal trainer provides: The client comes in and the trainer walks him through the session, providing instruction (1), they demonstrate the movements (2), correct the client's execution, (3) and maybe the most important of all: motivate the client to keep going (4). Many clients have landed in personal training because they could not bring themselves to go into a gym alone regularly. Also, pre-COVID, almost nobody had any fitness equipment (5) at home other than the cross-training machine that tended to act as more of an overpriced laundry rack (a not-so-decorative furniture piece whose only job was gathering dust).

With the shutdown of this major business sector, more and more people have explored and grown fond of the option to work out at home. Now, many people have invested in some equipment or rerouted to other options—for example—they now choose to work out outdoors instead.

This means that in 2020, the market was ripe for an offering that was not linked to a certain brick-and-mortar location with equipment. People were okay not seeing the coach in person. This will be true for many, many industries in the future as well. So, the time is ripe to leverage these new options.

If you feel like the pandemic has not done enough to "remotify" your industry, let's take a look at what you can do to move your career in that direction. Basically, any in-person interaction can be digitized in some form.

Start by assessing what the service provides to clients. (Like the numbered breakdown of the personal training job I included above). Then think about how these services could be provided in digital form, finding alternative ways to perform each service. To help you understand how to do this, let me show you how I digitalized all 5 parts of the personal training and coaching interactions in my business.

In the asynchronous, digital version of a personal training session, the instruction (1) and demonstration (2) are administered via an app where the exercises are found in videos, along with written instructions by the coach. The correction (3) happens via a video or photo the client can record and upload. The feedback loop is now not directly face-to-face or immediate, but more asynchronous. (The clients will only film a part of their workout, so that this task doesn't take away too much training time.) Feedback to the client is then provided by the coach via comments. For the last piece, the equipment (5), there are many ways to get someone in shape without any equipment at all.

For most clients, I found a good setup was already in their home before the pandemic. For a few, I recommended that they get 1 to 3 pieces of equipment to make their training more enjoyable, making sure these items would fit within a reasonable budget. If I had wished, I could've also pursued a joint venture with an equipment manufacturer to put together both minimum and optimum bundles at reduced, affiliate rates.

Another way to digitize a personal training session could be, instead of having the coach live beside you, to perform it via a Zoom call. With the cellular coverage nowadays, you can even take your Zoom call with the coach to a local gym. Just pop your wireless headphones in and prop up your phone. Neither of these versions require you to be physically there, though some rely on fixed business hours (if your person is working out in a gym that isn't open 24 hours)—you can choose when to do the work and align it with when you do your best work.

Making your job more adaptable to the 3/2 method starts with things we've outlined in earlier chapters, like getting more meetings online.

"Not the Same" Attracts Different Clients

Few of the asynchronous, digital services will be exactly the same as the traditional ones. But that is not inherently bad because it will target a new audience. It's a redeveloped, new offer. If your asynchronous offering sounds a little stark and you feel like "nobody will buy that," let's remember how shocked we were in 2008 when Apple delivered its first laptop and computer without CD/DVD drives. Now, it is difficult to find even desktops with any sort of disk drive.

The benefit the digital, personal training plan I used as an example provides is that what used to have a price point of $150 per session, can start at $250 to $350 per month and include 9 to 25 sessions. This is 9 to 12 as many training sessions for the same price! The client still gets the benefit of a tailored training plan, but it offers quicker improvements while still being able to target a certain area they want to work on.

Although the amount of feedback from the coach will be less, it won't be completely absent. As the success of a training program often not only hinges on particular exercises and their execution, but also pure number of total sessions and training consistently week after week, the client can get more bang for their buck by effectively getting 25 sessions instead of 2 out of the same monthly budget.

So, if you are stuck at a 5/2 workweek job and see no way out—think about how your area of work was digitized during the lockdown period—or could be further adjusted.

List the parts of the service you are currently offering and think about how they could be digitized. Then invest a step further: Ask yourself what other areas from the 3/2 method can be used to improve the talents, knowledge, and type of work that you do?

Scan QR Code for Worksheet: Tips for Making Your Job Asynchronous

Key Takeaways

- Any job can be dissected into the major services provided. We can then take each and every service and figure out how it can be done in a more asynchronous, remote, or digital way.
- You are not necessarily creating an exact copy, but by creating a new service (that you've adapted to be more remote) there might also be a new market segment for you to sell to.

CHAPTER 18

The End (Or Is It?)

For the majority of our society, there is nothing balanced about the way we work compared to how much free time we have. And even though our contract might say we get paid for working 40 hours, most are spending 10% to 50% more time than that at work—and still feel bad about leaving early or slotting in time for a much-needed doctor's appointment. But the proof is adding up: We are going down a one-way street lined with precarious roadblocks like deteriorating health and burnout.

The pandemic ripped the Pandora's box of work wide open: Even longer workdays are added upon ever-expanding stress, and blurring life-work boundaries leave us ignoring kids (or half-clothed spouses) for interruptions caused by "important" calls.

But there is hope: Studies done in New Zealand and statistics from Nordic countries show that we don't have to work long hours to be productive—and we are happier if we don't. We have proof of concept that the 4-day workweek does not mean we get less work done. Different versions of remote work can be the most productive forms of modern work if we leverage the benefits and handle the downsides well. The question is, after 100 years of working an old model, are we ready to change?

Are you willing to trust yourself to have 2 additional weekends every month and still have equal (or even improved) productivity? Are you sure it can really work for you? Well, if you weren't at least willing to try, you wouldn't be reading these words. And to prove that what I've been teaching about the 3/2 method really is productive, I want to let you in on a secret.

This book was written over a period of 9 months when I held a full-time job that entailed 2 major changes in my role. Within the same time frame, my partner and I renovated our whole apartment. We outsourced the kitchen and bathrooms, but to save money, we ripped down all our wallpaper, repainted, did all the tear-down work, and redid the floors ourselves.

Oh, and we also got a 6-month old puppy from the animal shelter whose house-breaking and basic education was 95% my duty. Except for the first and last month, I didn't even need to spend my free days or weekends on the book. We also took 4 weeks of vacation in the same time frame (with zero work on the book). And just in case you are following up on what I said: My average steps (according to my phone) were 7,350 and my daily workout average was 49 minutes a day for over 15 days a month. And although you have no clue how much work (blood, sweat, and tears) writing a book is, maybe you'll take my word for it that with the 3/2 model, everything I described, all happening at the same time, is possible.

It doesn't matter if you choose the rotating 3/2 workweek or the Wednesday-Off model. If you approach the 3/2 method with the mindset of leveraging what it has to offer—humongous productivity benefits, a wealth of happiness and life-balance, and the freedom to not be controlled by your work or work hours—the batching and pruning will work for you. And all without any need to get up at 4:00 am, push through 12-hour workdays, or log back in to your work accounts on your free days.

Does this sound too good to be true? It's not! The only thing standing between you thinking about switching to this model and achieving it is the doing. So, before you add this book to the pile of already-read but never-acted-on books, let me ask you a question. What is one 5-minute task you can do *right now* to take the first step into a happier, more productive life? Do it now. I'll tell my editor to cut out 5 minutes' worth of reading to make up for your time. (This is the editor speaking, and I got you those 5 minutes, cross my heart.) Maybe with those spare minutes you want to load and print one of the cheat sheets, or sign up for my newsletter so you'll get continued, helpful tips (hint-hint, check out www.3on2off.com/extras).

Did you do it? Did you use your 5 minutes?

That wasn't that hard, was it? The hardest thing was probably to getting over yourself so that you could start. Congratulations: You've taken the first step. The second step is for you to think of the second action that would get you set up on the right path. This can be a bigger one, a 20- or 60-minute task. I want you to plan it into your next 2 weeks. Open your trusty calendar and book a meeting with yourself. Make it 90 minutes including some buffer time.

Nice work.

Now you are practically on your journey to implementing your own 3/2 workweek. You are paving the way not only to a more productive you, but also a happier and healthier you. That's a big deal (get yourself a cookie or dance to your favorite song when we've finished to celebrate).

Let's leave no doubt: The future of the working world belongs to the well-balanced, healthy employees. The future has a high demand for anyone who can be creative, come up with new ideas, and deliver results. The era of time-stamping, pencil-pushing employees and helicopter bosses is over.

The world cares about the quality of your work, not the hours you put in. The productivity is the amount of work you can put into an hour, not how many work hours you can put into a day or a month. Highly skilled and capable employees *will* have all of the leverage in the future.

Now it's up to you to take action. If the worksheets provided are not your favorite form of learning, I have also put together an on-demand e-learning course so you can follow along. If you still feel stuck putting the 3/2 method into place, or can't figure out all the specific things that would help you level up your productivity, you can also hire me to mentor you through the process (or coach you through the hold-ups). We'll hop on a call to figure out what you need and if I can help you get there. If we decide we are a good fit to work together, I'll interview you about your current job and put together an action plan we can set into motion together.

You can also book me as a speaker or to head a workshop to motivate your team or company. I can help. To see these different options, please go to 3on2off.com/book to get started. I can't wait to talk to you.

Endnotes

1. Guy, Jack. "Employees Working from Home Are Putting in Longer Hours than before the Pandemic." CNN. Cable News Network, February 5, 2021. https://edition.cnn.com/2021/02/05/business/working-from-home-hours-pandemic-scli-intl-gbr/index.html.
2. IPS, Releaselive. "Work from Home Spikes on US Holidays." IPS Inter Press Service Business, December 4, 2020. https://ipsnews.net/business/2020/12/04/work-from-home-spikes-on-us-holidays.
3. "Mental Health in the Workplace." World Health Organization. World Health Organization. Accessed July 28, 2022. https://www.who.int/teams/mental-health-and-substance-use/promotion-prevention/mental-health-in-the-workplace.
4. Kelly, Jack. "Indeed Study Shows That Worker Burnout Is at Frighteningly High Levels: Here Is What You Need to Do Now." Forbes. Forbes Magazine, April 14, 2022. https://www.forbes.com/sites/jackkelly/2021/04/05/indeed-study-shows-that-worker-burnout-is-at-frighteningly-high-levels-here-is-what-you-need-to-do-now/?sh=37749b6c23bb.
5. Lin, Kuan-Han PhD, Chau-Chung Wu MD, PhD, Tzong-Shinn Chu MD, PhD, Tien-Shang Huang MD, and Yen-Yuan Chen MD, MPH, PhD. "Employer or Employee: Who Is More Likely to Suffer from... : Journal of Occupational and Environmental Medicine." Employer or Employee Who is More Likely to Suffer From Burnout? Journal of Occupational and

Environmental Medicine, April 2020. https://journals.lww.com/joem/Fulltext/2020/04000/Employer_or_Employee___Who_is_More_Likely_to_Suffer.13.a.

6. "Millennials at Work Reshaping the Workplace in Financial Services - PWC." Millennials at work Reshaping the workplace. PWC. Accessed July 28, 2022. https://www.pwc.com/gx/en/financial-services/publications/assets/pwc-millenials-at-work.pdf.
7. Mccrindle. "Gen Z and Gen Alpha Infographic Update." mccrindle, February 9, 2022. https://mccrindle.com.au/insights/blogarchive/gen-z-and-gen-alpha-infographic-update.
8. Stahl, Ashley. "How Gen-Z Is Bringing a Fresh Perspective to the World of Work." Forbes. Forbes Magazine, December 10, 2021. https://www.forbes.com/sites/ashleystahl/2021/05/04/how-gen-z-is-bringing-a-fresh-perspective-to-the-world-of-work/?sh=64c2a6a10c22.
9. Dyble, Mark, Jack Thorley, Abigail E. Page, Daniel Smith, and Andrea Bamberg Migliano. "Engagement in Agricultural Work Is Associated with Reduced Leisure Time among Agta Hunter-Gatherers." Nature News. Nature Publishing Group, May 20, 2019. https://www.nature.com/articles/s41562-019-0614-6.
10. Schor, Juliet B. Pre-industrial workers had a shorter workweek than today's. Massachusetts Institute of Technology. Accessed July 29, 2022. https://groups.csail.mit.edu/mac/users/rauch/worktime/hours_workweek.html.

From her book The Overworked American: The Unexpected Decline of Leisure

11. "Work Time and Employment (A Conference Report)." *National Commission for Manpower Policy* Special Report No. 28 (October 1978).
12. "Today in History - August 20." The Library of Congress. Accessed August 2, 2022. https://www.loc.gov/item/today-in-history/august-20.
13. Brinkley, Douglas. "80 Days That Changed the World." Time. Time Inc., March 31, 2003. http://content.time.com/time/specials/packages/article/0,28804,1977881_1977883_1977922,00.html.
14. "Today in History - August 20." The Library of Congress. Accessed August 2, 2022. https://www.loc.gov/item/today-in-history/august-20.
15. O'Neill, Aaron. "Europe: Cars per 1,000 Inhabitants 1914-1949, by Region." Statista, December 31, 2006. https://www.statista.com/statistics/1073212/europe-cars-per-thousand-people-by-region-historical.
16. Published by D. Clark. "Average Working Hours EU 2021." Statista, March 9, 2022. https://www.statista.com/statistics/1197097/average-working-hours-eu.
17. Kuhn, Peter, and Fernando Lozano. "The Expanding Workweek? Understanding Trends in Long Work Hours among U.S. Men, 1979-2004." NBER, December 26, 2005. https://www.nber.org/papers/w11895.
18. Hewlett, Sylvia Ann, and Carolyn Buck Luce. "Extreme Jobs: The Dangerous Allure of the 70-Hour Workweek." Harvard Business Review, August 21, 2014. https://hbr.org/2006/12/extreme-jobs-the-dangerous-allure-of-the-70-hour-workweek.
19. Guy, Jack. "Employees Working from Home Are Putting in Longer Hours than before the Pandemic." CNN. Cable

News Network, February 5, 2021. https://edition.cnn.com/2021/02/05/business/working-from-home-hours-pandemic-scli-intl-gbr/index.html.

20. DeFilippis, Evan, Stephen Michael Impink, Madison Singell, Jeffrey T. Polzer, and Raffaella Sadun. "Collaborating during Coronavirus: The Impact of Covid-19 on the ... - NBER." Collaborating During Coronavirus: The Impact of COVID-19 on the Nature of Work. NBER Working Paper Series. Accessed August 2, 2022. https://www.nber.org/system/files/working_papers/w27612/w27612.pdf.
21. Owl Labs. *State of Remote Work 2021*. Somerville, MA: Owl Labs, 2021.
    5th annual edition.
22. Cook, Daniel. "Rules of Productivity Presentation." LOSTGARDEN Home. LOSTGARDEN, September 30, 2019. https://lostgarden.home.blog/2008/09/28/rules-of-productivity-presentation.
23. The Redbooth Team. November 15th. "Everybody's Working for the Weekend, but When Do You Actually Get Work Done?" Redbooth. Accessed August 3, 2022. https://redbooth.com/blog/your-most-productive-time.
24. Organisation for Economic Co-operation and Development. *Productivity - Level of GDP per capita and productivity*. OCED, November 16,2021.
25. Dembe, A E, J B Erikson, R G Delbos, and S M Banks. "The Impact of Overtime and Long Work Hours on Occupational Injuries and Illnesses: New Evidence from the United States." BMJ Journals | Occupational & Environmental Medicine, August 18, 2005. https://oem.bmj.com/content/62/9/588.

26. Pega, Frank, Bálint Náfrádi, Natalie C. Momen, Yuka Ujita, Kai N. Streicher, Annette M. Prüss-Üstün, Alexis Descatha, et al. "Global, Regional, and National Burdens of Ischemic Heart Disease and Stroke Attributable to Exposure to Long Working Hours for 194 Countries, 2000–2016: A Systematic Analysis from the WHO/ILO Joint Estimates of the Work-Related Burden of Disease and Injury." Science Direct. Environment International, May 17, 2021. https://www.sciencedirect.com/science/article/pii/S0160412021002208.
27. Kawakami, N., S. Araki, N. Takatsuka, H. Shimizu, and H. Ishibashi. "Overtime, Psychosocial Working Conditions, and Occurrence of Non- Insulin Dependent Diabetes Mellitus in Japanese Men." *Journal of Epidemiology & Community Health* 53, no. 6 (1999): 359–63. https://doi.org/10.1136/jech.53.6.359.
28. M, Shields. "Long Working Hours and Health." Health reports. U.S. National Library of Medicine. Accessed August 16, 2022. https://pubmed.ncbi.nlm.nih.gov/10618741.
29. Virtanen, Marianna, Markus Jokela, Solja T Nyberg, Ida E H Madsen, Tea Lallukka, Kirsi Ahola, Lars Alfredsson, et al. "Long Working Hours and Alcohol Use: Systematic Review and Meta-Analysis of Published Studies and Unpublished Individual Participant Data." The BMJ. British Medical Journal Publishing Group, January 13, 2015. https://www.bmj.com/content/350/bmj.g7772.
30. Hu, Nien-Chih, Jong-Dar Chen, and Tsun-Jen Cheng. "The Associations Between Long Working Hours, Physical Inactivity, and Burnout: Journal of Occupational and Environmental Medicine." The Associations

Between Long Working Hours, Physical Inactivity, and Burnout. Journal of Occupational and Environmental Medicine, May 2016. https://doi.org/10.1097/JOM.0000000000000715.

31. "Status of Working Hours and Mental Health Measures." MHLW. Accessed August 16, 2022. https://www.mhlw.go.jp/wp/hakusyo/karoushi/20/dl/20-1.pdf.
32. "The World Happiness Report." Home | The World Happiness Report. Sustainable Development Solutions Network. Accessed August 16, 2022. https://worldhappiness.report.
33. Organisation for Economic Co-operation and Development. *Productivity - Level of GDP per capita and productivity*. OCED, November 16,2021.
34. de Bloom, Jessica, Sabine A.E. Geurts, Toon W. Taris, Sabine Sonnentag, Carolina de Weerth, and Michiel A.J. Kompier. "Effects of Vacation from Work on Health and Well-Being: Lots of Fun, Quickly Gone." *Work & Stress* 24, no. 2 (2010): 196–216. https://doi.org/10.1080/02678373.2010.493385.
35. Westman, M., and D. Eden. "Effects of a Respite from Work on Burnout: Vacation Relief and Fade-out." American Psychological Association. American Psychological Association, 1997. https://psycnet.apa.org/doiLanding?doi=10.1037%2F0021-9010.82.4.516.
36. "Millennials at Work. Reshaping the Workplace." Millennials at work. PWC, 2011. https://www.pwc.com/co/es/publicaciones/assets/millennials-at-work.pdf.
37. Gilchrist, Karen. "Chatbots Expected to Cut Business Costs by $8 Billion by 2022." CNBC. CNBC, May 9, 2017. https://www.cnbc.com/2017/05/09/

chatbots-expected-to-cut-business-costs-by-8-billion-by-2022.html.

38. Schulte, Brigid. "Work Interruptions Can Cost You 6 Hours a Day. an Efficiency Expert Explains How to Avoid Them." The Washington Post. WP Company, October 27, 2021. https://www.washingtonpost.com/news/inspired-life/wp/2015/06/01/interruptions-at-work-can-cost-you-up-to-6-hours-a-day-heres-how-to-avoid-them.
39. Levels, Pieter. "There Will Be 1 Billion Digital Nomads by 2035." Levels.io. @levelsio (Pieter Levels), November 10, 2020. https://levels.io/future-of-digital-nomads/.
40. Bloom, Nicholas A., James Liang, John Roberts, and Zhichun Jenny Ying. "Does Working from Home Work? Evidence from a Chinese Experiment." Stanford Graduate School of Business. Stanford Graduate School of Business, March 1, 2013. https://www.gsb.stanford.edu/faculty-research/working-papers/does-working-home-work-evidence-chinese-experiment.
41. Owl Labs. *State of Remote Work 2021*. Somerville, MA: Owl Labs, 2021.
42. "The Evolving Office: Empower Employees to Work Vibrantly in 2022." The Evolving Office. Ergotron. Accessed August 17, 2022. https://www.ergotron.com/en-us/markets/office/work-vibrantly.
43. Perpetual Guardian, Coulthard Barnes, The University of Auckland, Auckland University of Technology, and MinterEllisonRuddWatts. "The Four-Day Week. Guidelines for an Outcome-Based Trial - Raising Productivity and Engagement. ." 4 Day Week Global. Perpetual Guardian, 2019. https://www.4dayweek.com.

44. Haraldsson, G., and J. Kellam. "Going Public: Iceland's Journey to a Shorter Working Week." Autonomy, July 14, 2021. https://autonomy.work/portfolio/icelandsww/.
45. Perpetual Guardian, Coulthard Barnes, The University of Auckland, Auckland University of Technology, and MinterEllisonRuddWatts. "The Four-Day Week. Guidelines for an Outcome-Based Trial - Raising Productivity and Engagement." 4 Day Week Global. Perpetual Guardian, 2019. https://www.4dayweek.com/.
46. Barnes, Andrew, and Stephanie Jones. *The 4 Day Week: How the Flexible Work Revolution Can Increase Productivity, Profitability and Well-Being, and Help Create a Sustainable Future*. London: Piatkus, 2020.
47. Duranton, Gilles, and Matthew A. Turner. "The Fundamental Law of Road Congestion: Evidence from US Cities." National Bureau of Economic Research. NBER, September 24, 2009. https://www.nber.org/papers/w15376.
48. Perpetual Guardian, Coulthard Barnes, The University of Auckland, Auckland University of Technology, and MinterEllisonRuddWatts. "The Four-Day Week. Guidelines for an Outcome-Based Trial - Raising Productivity and Engagement. ." 4 Day Week Global. Perpetual Guardian, 2019. https://www.4dayweek.com/.
49. Golden, Lonnie, Julia Henly, and Susan Lambert. "Work Schedule Flexibility for Workers: A Path to Employee Happiness?" *SSRN Electronic Journal*, 2012. https://doi.org/10.2139/ssrn.2129520.
50. Perpetual Guardian, Coulthard Barnes, The University of Auckland, Auckland University of Technology, and MinterEllisonRuddWatts. "The Four-Day Week.

Guidelines for an Outcome-Based Trial - Raising Productivity and Engagement." 4 Day Week Global. Perpetual Guardian, 2019. https://www.4dayweek.com.

51. Rand, David G., and Anna Dreber, Tore Ellingsen, Drew Fudenberg, and Matrin A. Nowak. Harvard University. "Carrots Are Better Than Sticks For Building Human Cooperation, Study Finds." ScienceDaily, Accessed August 18, 2022. www.sciencedaily.com/releases/2009/09/090903163550.htm.
52. The Redbooth Team. November 15th. "Everybody's Working for the Weekend, but When Do You Actually Get Work Done?" Redbooth. Accessed August 3, 2022. https://redbooth.com/blog/your-most-productive-time.
53. Binnewies, Carmen, Sabine Sonnentag, and Eva J. Mojza. "Recovery during the Weekend and Fluctuations in Weekly Job Performance: A Week-Level Study Examining Intra-Individual Relationships." *Journal of Occupational and Organizational Psychology* 83, no. 2 (2010): 419–41. https://doi.org/10.1348/096317909x418049.
54. "Millennials at Work. Reshaping the Workplace." Millennials at work. PWC, 2011. https://www.pwc.com/co/es/publicaciones/assets/millennials-at-work.pdf.
55. Perpetual Guardian, Coulthard Barnes, The University of Auckland, Auckland University of Technology, and MinterEllisonRuddWatts. "The Four-Day Week. Guidelines for an Outcome-Based Trial - Raising Productivity and Engagement. ." 4 Day Week Global. Perpetual Guardian, 2019. https://www.4dayweek.com/.
56. Newport, Cal. *Deep Work: Rules for Focused Success in a Distracted World*. New York: Grand Central Publishing, 2016.

57. "World's Heaviest Pumpkin." Guinness World Records. Accessed August 18, 2022. https://www.guinnessworldrecords.com/world-records/heaviest-pumpkin#:~:text=A%20pumpkin%20weighing%201%2C226%20kg,Italy%2C%20on%2026%20September%202021.
58. Owl Labs. *State of Remote Work 2021*. Somerville, MA: Owl Labs, 2021.
5th annual edition.
59. Perpetual Guardian, Coulthard Barnes, The University of Auckland, Auckland University of Technology, and MinterEllisonRuddWatts. "The Four-Day Week. Guidelines for an Outcome-Based Trial - Raising Productivity and Engagement. ." 4 Day Week Global. Perpetual Guardian, 2019. https://www.4dayweek.com/.
60. Boogaard, Kat. "How to Overcome Parkinson's Law." Work Life by Atlassian. Atlassian, March 17, 2022. https://www.atlassian.com/blog/productivity/what-is-parkinsons-law#:~:text=Parkinson's%20Law%20is%20the%20old,%E2%80%9CThe%20Economist%E2%80%9D%20in%201955.
61. CFI Team. "Pareto Efficiency." Corporate Finance Institute, February 3, 2021. https://corporatefinanceinstitute.com/resources/knowledge/economics/pareto-efficiency.
62. Reid, Erin. "Why Some Men Pretend to Work 80-Hour Weeks." Harvard Business Review, December 5, 2017. https://hbr.org/2015/04/why-some-men-pretend-to-work-80-hour-weeks.
63. Binnewies, Carmen, Sabine Sonnentag, and Eva J. Mojza. "Recovery during the Weekend

and Fluctuations in Weekly Job Performance: A Week-Level Study Examining Intra-Individual Relationships." *Journal of Occupational and Organizational Psychology* 83, no. 2 (2010): 419–41. https://doi.org/10.1348/096317909x418049.

64. Sonnentag, S., and S. Jelden. "Job Stressors and the Pursuit of Sport Activities: A Day-Level Perspective." Journal of Occupational Health Psychology. American Psychological Association, 2009. https://doi.apa.org/doiLanding?doi=10.1037%2Fa0014953.
65. Dijksterhuis, Ap, and Loran F. Nordgren. "A Theory of Unconscious Thought." *Perspectives on Psychological Science* 1, no. 2 (2006): 95–109. https://doi.org/10.1111/j.1745-6916.2006.00007.x.
66. Binnewies, Carmen, Sabine Sonnentag, and Eva J. Mojza. "Recovery during the Weekend and Fluctuations in Weekly Job Performance: A Week-Level Study Examining Intra-Individual Relationships." *Journal of Occupational and Organizational Psychology* 83, no. 2 (2010): 419–41. https://doi.org/10.1348/096317909x418049.
67. Keller, Gary, and Jay Papasan. *The ONE Thing: The Surprisingly Simple Truth Behind Extraordinary Results.* Austin, Texas: Bard Press, 2021.
68. Kaplan, Rachel, and Stephen Kaplan. *The Experience of Nature: A Psychological Perspective.* Cambridge: Cambridge University Press, 1989.
69. Ginoux, Clement, Sandrine Isoard-Gautheur, and Philippe Sarrazin. "'What Did You Do This Weekend?" Relationships between Weekend Activities, Recovery Experiences, and Changes in Work-Related Well-Being."

Applied Psychology. Health and Well-Being. U.S. National Library of Medicine. Accessed August 25, 2022. https://pubmed.ncbi.nlm.nih.gov/33864428/.

70. Sonnentag, S., and S. Jelden. "Job Stressors and the Pursuit of Sport Activities: A Day-Level Perspective." Journal of Occupational Health Psychology. American Psychological Association, 2009. https://doi.apa.org/doiLanding?doi=10.1037%2Fa0014953.

71. Lee, I-Min, Eric J. Shiroma, Masamitsu Kamada, David R. Bassett, Charles E. Matthews, and Julie E. Buring. "Association of STEP Volume and Intensity with All-Cause Mortality in Older Women." *JAMA Internal Medicine* 179, no. 8 (2019): 1105. https://doi.org/10.1001/jamainternmed.2019.0899.

72. Paluch, Amanda E., Kelley Pettee Gabriel, Janet E. Fulton, Cora E. Lewis, Pamela J. Schreiner, Barbara Sternfeld, Stephen Sidney, Juned Siddique, Kara M. Whitaker, and Mercedes R. Carnethon. "Steps per Day and All-Cause Mortality in Middle-Aged Adults in the Coronary Artery Risk Development in Young Adults Study." *JAMA Network Open* 4, no. 9 (2021). https://doi.org/10.1001/jamanetworkopen.2021.24516.

73. Ballin, Marcel, Oskar Antonsson, Viktor Rosenqvist, Peter Nordström, and Anna Nordström. "Association of Dog Ownership with Accelerometer-Measured Physical Activity and Daily Steps in 70-Year-Old Individuals: A Population-Based Cross-Sectional Study." *BMC Public Health*, 2313, 21, no. 1 (2021). https://doi.org/10.1186/s12889-021-12401-4.

74. "Improving Sleep: A Guide to a Good Night's Rest." Harvard Health, 2019. https://www.health.harvard.

edu/staying-healthy/improving-sleep-a-guide-to-a-good-nights-rest#excerpt.

75. Chaput, Jean-Philippe, Caroline Dutil, Ryan Featherstone, Robert Ross, Lora Giangregorio, Travis J. Saunders, Ian Janssen, et al. "Sleep Duration and Health in Adults: An Overview of Systematic Reviews." *Applied Physiology, Nutrition, and Metabolism* 45, no. 10 (Suppl. 2) (2020): S218–S231. https://doi.org/10.1139/apnm-2020-0034.

Acknowledgements

Make sure you read the last paragraph (because it refers to you, yes YOU, the one reading this). First, a tip of the hat for those that made my life hard and frustrated me with their methods (or lack thereof). That part of my story lit a fire under my butt not to become the same type of person, employee, or leader they were. They inspired me to search for other methods than theirs (better than the ones that never worked for me) and one of those paths led me to all the solutions found in this book.

I consider myself very lucky I was able to work under Ralf Manok. Thank you, Ralf. You taught me how to ride the lion (and sell Easter bunnies under a ludicrous deadline) long before becoming an entrepreneur ever crossed my mind. But most importantly, you taught me that having fun and working hard don't need to be mutually exclusive. You also showed me that no matter how high the demands of the big bosses upstairs are, there is a limit where we employees should say "No" and just call it a day.

My gratitude also belongs to my mentor, Ken Andrukow. You were the first business owner I encountered that strictly adhered to a 4-day week—long before it ever became popular. You showed me it was possible. The origin of this book stems from our many talks on how to improve productivity and prevent overwork as an entrepreneur.

Many thanks to my company ActiveLifeRX, my co-workers, and especially its founder Dr. Sean Pastuch, who fully embraced the remote working environment. In all honesty, I became a fan long before I became a staff member. The education you provided enabled me to see a way to form my job and business into a sustainable remote working environment. My gratitude also belongs to my direct manager, Dr. Ryan Summers, who showed nothing but genuine interest and support in my crazy working model and even crazier idea to write this book.

This book also wouldn't have been possible without the path others paved before me and the road they laid down. From the great analogy for pruning in Mike Michalowicz's The Pumpkin Plan, to the productivity gurus David Allen, Cal Newport, and Henry Ford—I am indebted to your work, as mine is based on what you have already found to be true. I merely had to pick up where you left off and develop these concepts further. We stand on the shoulders of the giants who came before us, so my short 5'5" self is thankful I got that lift.

Bringing a book to life is a lot more than just typing up words. A big thanks for the help of my marketing strategist Patti Zorr for spearheading the process, the marketing strategy, and assembling a great publishing team to bring this book together. A big thank you also goes to editor Kristin Spencer from Literary Symmetry for her patience and diligence while working on my manuscript. You not only made it easier to read, but also more enjoyable (I laughed out loud at times) which is more than I could have ever asked for.

A big thank you goes to my closer support network of family and friends. To Katrin and Nadja for your generous support and genuine interest in the book's content as well as progress. To my parents, who wrestled with the bumpy first drafts and were determined to troubleshoot my ideas until they all made sense. Thank you.

I couldn't have done or come up with a lot that makes the 3 on, 2 off method what it is today without my wife. Thank you for your support. Like letting me type on long car rides or bury my nose in the phone when my publishing team had questions. Thank you for having my back.

And lastly, I want to thank you, my reader. Thank you for letting me be a part of your life and journey. Let's stay in touch! You can find me on Instagram, Facebook, and Twitter if you search for "Linda Morgi." Please keep me updated on how your productivity journey goes and let me know if there is anything else I can help you with.

And now, it's time to put the book down and get to work. You've got this.

Book Linda to Speak

Book Linda to speak at your event and she is guaranteed to deliver you an entertaining and inspiring speech targeted to your audience and everyone's goals. Next to keeping them engaged, her main goal is to create immediate, actionable steps for your team and company.

With over 15 years of public speaking experience, she'll have your guests laughing and feeling inspired by her true stories.

Spearhead your new productive working schedule or empower your team to greater results with Linda as your next keynote speaker.

For more information visit: 3on2off.com

About the Author

Linda Morgi is a reformed hustle-culture enthusiast, a fitness and health expert, and an inspirational speaker. When she isn't coaching or speaking, she specializes in helping her clients get wins with her signature holistic approach that cuts through the noise of life by offering practical solutions.

After a career in consumer goods companies like Kraft, Danone, and Apple, Linda became an entrepreneur in the health and fitness space. In addition to coaching in the fitness arena to help her clients reduce their physical pain, she also mentors coaches from all around the world to help them find a better work-life balance.

Linda calls both Switzerland and Germany home and lives with her wife and two dogs. When she isn't geeking out on Latte Art, she keeps herself fit by working out in her garage gym, going biking outdoors, or heading out for a climb.

You can find more from Linda on her website lindamorgi.com, and you can also follow her on Instagram @lindamorgi.

Printed in Great Britain
by Amazon

20813913R00159